# Dilemmas of
# Modern Religious Life

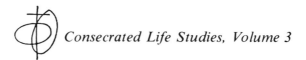 *Consecrated Life Studies, Volume 3*

# Dilemmas of
# Modern Religious Life

*by*

*J. M. R. Tillard, O.P.*

## Michael Glazier, Inc.
Wilmington, Delaware

## About the Author

J.M.R. Tillard, O.P., is Professor of Divinity at the Faculte de Theologie in Ottawa. He received his doctorate in philosophy from the Universite Angelicum and his doctorate in theology from the Universite le-Saulchoir. Among his many publications are *One in Christ* and *The Bishop of Rome*.

English translation of *Appel du Christ...Appels du monde: Les religieux relisent leur appel* (©Les Edition du Cerf, 1978) first published in 1984 by Michael Glazier, Inc., 1723 Delaware Avenue, Wilmington, Delaware 19806

English translation ©1984 by Michael Glazier, Inc. All rights reserved.

Library of Congress Card Catalog Number: 84-81253
International Standard Book Numbers:
   *Consecrated Life Studies* series: 0-89453-379-7
   DILEMMAS: 0-89453-446-7

Cover design by Lillian Brulc

Printed in the United States of America

# CONTENTS

# CHAPTER I

# Religious Life and Work

A characteristic feature of the religious life as it has developed over the past fifteen years has been the choice by religious of new forms of involvement with what we may call the "working world". Such a choice has frequently resulted in their joining movements for the promotion of social justice, and their consequent engagement at times, and in varying degrees, in political activity.

Up to the present, religious congregations have, with rare exceptions, been accustomed to assign their members to work of an institutional nature — in colleges, schools, hospitals, for example, which either belonged to them or had been committed to their care by the church or by the state. Members of religious congregations labored in such employments for the good of all the world's people — believers and unbelievers alike — but in settings which remained avowedly church-centered, Christian, in a word "religious". Very often, they tried to make the places of their apostolic labor extensions, as it were, of their communities; and that is why a special climate prevailed in their schools and hospitals — a concern for people as persons and a conscientious attention to duty which are not too often found in secular institutions.

More and more, however, and at an ever-increasing rate, religious are teaching in state schools, working as nurses in public hospitals, tending the elderly and infirm at home, and thus performing on the outside the work which they had previously done within their own establishments. Others make a more radical choice and seek out a profession or a trade which has no affinity to — much less any direct connection with — the work which their congregation has always regarded as its secondary object, or at least its specific type of activity. Women religious drive trucks, work as restaurant cooks, practice as engineers or lawyers. The range of the jobs they take includes almost every ordinary trade and profession, and they have a particular preference for occupations which allow them the closest contact with working people regarded as a class.

This new trend, and the theological rethinking (more or less implicit) which underlies it, are much more important and are likely to have greater consequences than other changes in the religious life over the last quarter-century which have caught the popular imagination and have occasioned violent controversy at times. The new trend and its basis in theology indicate a considerable evolution in the concept of what the mission of religious should be among the people of God. If there is a vast distance between the first timid experiments of the "Worker Religious" after World War II and the decisions made at recent chapter meetings of many religious congregations, it is owing not only to changes in the kind of work undertaken by religious but is above all the result of a change in theological perspective. It is not enough for us merely to note this as a fact. We must reflect upon it in depth.

## WHY THIS INVOLVEMENT?

First of all, the question of motivation must be cleared up. Theologians have been slow to deal with it. Disapproving critics of the new forms of involvement fail, as a rule, to ask what moves religious to take such decisions. Yet this is the very crux of the matter. Why do congregations opt to work in new surroundings and even in new kinds of work, often at the cost of difficult adjustments? Fifteen years ago, the answer to that question might well have been that circumstances compelled it. Very often, the choice was a pragmatic one — like heading for an exit in an emergency. On the one hand, the number of novices entering congregations had fallen off while the number of those leaving had swelled. In view of this, many institutions were closed or merged. Otherwise, the few youthful religious would have become either passive onlookers while a particular kind of apostolic activity inched its way to extinction, or else have been driven to desperation by having the whole weight of the congregation's work imposed on them — as if they were the apex of an inverted pyramid. Then too, in many countries, the state had assumed charge of activities (teaching, youth work, hospitals) in which religious congregations previously had worked. Some other employment had to be sought for the youngest religious and for those of middle-age who had become redundant. Short of changing the specific purpose and aim of a congregation, or turning every house into a shelter for the prematurely retired, some means had to be found whereby its members could continue to live in its spirit and pursue its proper work outside of institutions which were under its direct control.

However, even where external pressures have prevailed and played a key role in effecting change, they are no longer the dominant motivation. To be sure, they are still to be reckoned with but they have been absorbed into a theological restudy of the Church's mission. Proof of this is to be found in the decisions taken at recent chapter meetings dealing with renewal; for the most part care has been taken to base such decisions on a coherent, doctrinal vision. They are no longer decided on for purely pragmatic reasons nor by the determination to continue at all costs the pursuit of a congregation's "secondary aim". As I see it, this is a very important development.

*A New Relationship to the World*

Since Vatican II, religious have not confined their efforts at *aggiornamento* to its bare necessities. They have tried to accomplish it in close communion with the quest of the entire Church and have made it a rule to conduct their own reform in the full spirit of that reconsideration of the Church's life and mission which the people of God have embarked upon. This explains why *Perfectae Caritatis* has gradually come to be interpreted in the spirit of *Gaudium et Spes*, even though it was originally conceived and composed within the perspectives of *Lumen Gentium*. This remarkable fact has received too little attention. The missionary perspectives of the *Constitution of the Church in the Modern World* have filled up the horizon to such an extent that one of the principal thrusts of renewal on the part of religious congregations — as well as by local churches and Christian groups generally — has been a search for new ways of relating to the world in the interest, essentially, of evangelization.

The germ of this reorientation existed in the conciliar discussions concerning the document *Adaptation and Renovation of the Religious Life*, if not in the document itself. If you read today, with the benefit of hindsight, the list of interventions by bishops and superiors during the council sessions and the modifications they asked for, you cannot fail to be struck by the awareness shown of the apostolate — of the need for dedication in the service of the mission. In view of the dechristianization of whole countries which once were firm in the Faith, this was a theme which had been pondered over to some extent for a number of years. A mobilization of the entire Church was needed for furtherance of this apostolic commitment. *Gaudium et Spes* gave it a new dimension, and it has come to take priority in the thinking of congregations devoted to the active life — to say nothing of its impact on monks and contemplatives — and to dominate their reconsideration of what was required of them.

Two paragraphs of *Gaudium et Spes* have been decisive.

They are paragraphs 42 and 43. They are long and too dense; one wishes today that they were at once more explicit and more tentative. But at the end of the council they threw wide open a door which until then had been left timidly only a bit ajar. The apostolic exhortation of Paul VI on evangelization (8 December, 1975), repeated their essentials with remarkable fidelity. We must here quote a few lines, which touch on the heart of our subject:

> (30) The Church is in duty bound — as her bishops have insisted — to proclaim the liberation of these hundreds of millions of people since very many of them are her children. She has the duty of helping this liberation, of bearing witness on its behalf and of assuring its full development. All this is in no way irrelevant to evangelization.
>
> (31) In fact there are close links between evangelization and human advancement — that is, development and liberation. There is a connection in the anthropological order because the one who is to be evangelized is not an abstract being but a person subject to social and economic factors. There is also a connection in the theological sphere because the plan of creation cannot be isolated from the plan of redemption which extends to the very practical question of eradicating injustice and establishing justice. There is, finally, a connection in the evangelical order — that is, the order of charity: for how can the new law be proclaimed unless it promotes true advancement of man in a spirit of justice and peace? (Evangelii Nuntiandi, nos. 30, 31. Translation from *Evangelization Today*, published with commentary by Dominican Publications.)

Guided by this new light, the post-conciliar Church has rethought its nature and its mission, turning away from the light that had guided it in recent centuries and which saw the birth of many religious families. At the same time, under the inspiration of the council, religious discovered that their apostolic vocation could not be truly achieved except in total acceptance of what the Church as a whole took as its missionary objective. Reform became impossible for them, therefore, unless it corresponded closely with the Church's rethinking of its apostolic responsibility. It is this desire to be faithful to one's mission, and to take account of the link between evangelization and human advancement, which explains the new involvement of religious men and women in the world of work. At the root of the decisions of recent chapters there is the desire to "proclaim the new commandment" by joining in people's efforts to secure the reign of justice and peace. These decisions are the echo, the effect of the Church's new perception of its mission.

It is not a question then — as it has been wrongly claimed — of a "conversion to the service of the world and of man". Such service has always been the aim and the achievement of religious no matter what habit they wore or what their obedience, even if they did not proclaim it from the rooftops. The monks, for example, with their land, their workshops and their libraries did no less for humanity than did the tenants, the peasants, the laborers and the lay scholars of their time. The same is true of teaching or nursing congregations; even of humble service of which even the simplest person was capable. But in order to locate their *aggiornamento* within the missionary thrust of the post-conciliar Church, the congregations have nevertheless had to find another "place" for the tasks which up to now had been theirs or which they had felt it proper to add to their activity.

## Finding Another "Place" for Mission

The more we reflect on this problem, the clearer it becomes that, in essence, everything is staked on it; and all the more so since this quest is inseparable from the desire to redefine separation or seclusion from the world. The *fuga mundi* — which has its justification within the thrust of *Gaudium et Spes* — is given concrete expression in the life-style of religious of every kind, from the way they dress and the places they live in, to how they are formed and educated to "follow Christ". The impulse to find new kinds of work, leading usually to the choice of purely secular employment in a secular milieu and among men and women of every sort, arises in the main — one might even say it finds its ultimate reason — in the desire on the part of religious families, especially those of the "active life", to find a new "place" for their apostolic activity.

In this context, what is meant by "another place"? It is obvious that we are not speaking of a place in the geographical sense, of moving from a place inside the community institution to another outside the community institution. What is in question is a "place" in keeping with evangelization in the sense described in the passage of *Evangelii Nuntiandi* already quoted. Among the qualities possessed by such a "place", a link with human advancement and liberation and especially a bias towards justice would predominate. This would imply that one could not easily imagine any "place" other than where people lead their secular lives. Basically, the "very practical question of eradicating injustice" and the "social and economic factors" which have bearing on the liberation of mankind are encountered in their concrete reality in the secular sphere of daily existence and not in the sphere of the religious life. Without denying that (sad to say) injustice is to be found there too, religious milieux or the activities and institutions attached to them are not of their nature theaters for the deployment of vast efforts to achieve liberation.

The "place" sought, therefore, ought to be on the bare soil where tomorrow's humanity ferments and germinates in all its complexity. Or, perhaps in the work-yards and shops where a world is being built, with all their unavoidable cultural and socio-political dimensions. It is not in the least surprising that the need was felt to move gradually — aided by circumstances, let it be said — from the apostolate proper to a congregation but exercised in a circumscribed religious or ecclesial ambit, to an apostolate in the secular sphere in the company of all sorts of people, believers and unbelievers. Clearly, the principal motivation was mission. It is also clear that re-examination of the task prescribed by the founder's charism was not a search for an easy way out or a refusal to meet needs, but was conducted in the context of the reassessment which the people of God was making of its responsibility.

It may perhaps be objected that such a "place", since it belongs to the profane and secular areas of human life, has no direct link with the traditional "following of Christ", properly understood. Is not the following of Christ — *sequela Christi* — necessarily "religious", if not in its primary purpose, at least in the forms in which that purpose expresses itself? Are we not rediscovering today that the origins of oriental monasticism — of all Christian monasticism — are essentially "religious"?

## *The Mission of Active Religious Life*

This objection must be taken seriously. The answer cannot be exactly the same, however, for monks and contemplatives, for orders engaged in pastoral work for the Christian community, and for congregations involved in apostolic or charitable tasks. The demands of a Cistercian life or of a Dominican life faithful to the intuition of their founders are not at all points identical with those of a Little Brother of Charles de Foucauld or a Little Sister of the Assumption. This is too often forgotten.

In the light of such reflections, it would seem wrong to make too rigid a distinction — as has been done in recent years — between the type of apostolic activity which is proper to active religious congregations and that which is proper to lay apostles. In times past, when the laity were denied that apostolic responsibility as part of the people of God which is now seen as theirs, pious men and women, a good part of whom were lay people, did not hesitate to become involved wherever the service of the Church demanded it. They acted, it must be understood, in the context of the categories of their times. Priests, monks and nuns consecrated their lives to the liberation of captives from the Muslims. They became hotel-keepers, built cities, taught Western skills to Africans. And they felt at one with them. Today's options must be considered from the same viewpoint. It is wrong to think that there is an apostolic zone reserved to the laity and forbidden to religious. This is true even for involvement with trade unions, provided it is in harmony with the other components of a religious commitment.

Religious, in effect, "follow Christ" throughout all His domain but this must not be understood to refer merely to that *other world*, which will come into being on the day that Christ will deliver the Kingdom to the Father (1 Cor 15:24-28). It refers as well to this world which is destined to be a changed world, a *world made other* — that is, a world where humanity will appear as God destined it to be, sustained in peace, justice and mutual love. According to the Gospel, Jesus connects the coming of the Kingdom with the accomplishment of acts which will serve as signs — acts against everything that oppresses mankind and shadows his life on earth. To pull down the curtain on suffering, to knock down the walls of hatred, to make a little more justice and peace possible on this earth — in a word, to work for the "true advancement of man" in dignity is objectively to serve God, to establish the Kingdom of which now      until he shall have delivered it to the Father    Jesus Christ is Lord.

This is true even if the name of the God of Jesus Christ is not pronounced in the course of this service, for it is done before God and in accordance with His will, which is that this world should become *other*. He alone is the judge of such things. It is not primarily the reaction of people one looks for in performing this service, even if they are its beneficiaries. The primary object is not to win over another person, to put him in mind of God or the Kingdom so that he or she will aspire towards the other world. The object is first of all to obey the will of the Lord for this world. Of course, just as the will of God for this *world made other* is inextricably bound up with His will for the *other world*, whatever a Christian does for this present world tends towards witness to Christ and to His Father. From the very start, the primary intention behind such service is to collaborate in the transformation of this world so as to bring it into harmony with the already existing intimations of the

Kingdom. It is, let us repeat, an action *before* God.

The secondary aim of the religious congregations founded in recent centuries fits squarely into this approach. To educate poor children, to nurse the sick, bring up orphans, instruct underdeveloped peoples in the progress of technology — all the acts of evangelical charity planned by male and female founders — are an involvement before God for the sake of mankind. It would be to caricature the intentions of the founders to see these activities, for whose sake very often the institutes were founded, as attempts to capture people's good will, *captatio benevolentiae*, their sole purpose being to persuade them to listen to the revelation of Jesus Christ. With very rare exceptions, the documents concerning the origins of these congregations present the activities, not as a way of announcing Christ, but as a way of living the Gospel. When Vincent de Paul cared for poor children, it was not primarily in order thus to preach the faith. He did it in the first place in order to live, in the situation facing him, the charity of Christ. His witness is the brilliant evidence of a selfless fidelity to the Gospel, *before* God. This *before* God is primary. It is the same for every active religious congregation.

Of course, there are no religious faithful to their vocation who do not long for the day when they can proclaim the name of Christ, thus pointing to the One who, they believe, is the only source of the fullness of happiness for men and women and for the world. This desire to preach the Gospel explicitly is even more pronounced, ordinarily, among religious than it is among lay apostles. These usually feel themselves called more to a witness of solidarity with people who spend their lives in the pursuit of justice than to preach Jesus Christ and they are content with this, certain that this is what the Spirit is asking of them. Religious, however, feel that they have gone but halfway towards meeting their responsibilities if they have not preached Christ, have not unveiled the full content of their faith. The following of Christ includes announcing Him whom one follows. At the same time, even if religious find themselves in a position where they cannot speak of what they believe, even if there is nobody to understand the reason for their activities, even if a long period of silent presence is required before the name of the Lord Jesus can be pronounced, they will still feel constrained to work to change the world along the lines of the Gospel. It is something due to God, a responsibility laid upon them *before* God from the very fact that they "follow Christ" throughout all His domain. Doing this, they do not betray their vocation. If the entire world had no further need to hear the Gospel message, because it had heard and accepted it, religious would still be bound to accomplish the secondary aim of their congregations. There would still be need to make this world a little more *other*. There would still be injustices to be redressed, physical and moral hurt to be healed in the charity of the Gospel. Were not many congregations founded during times of greatest pious fervor in order to perform the works of mercy in the Christian community?

## Concern with the Long-Term

A concern with the "long-term" is the reason why religious congregations have extended their choice of activities and why they involve themselves at the heart of the working world — why they have gone from a religious "place" of work to a secular "place", and from charitable activities to activities implying solidarity with movements for the liberation and progress of humanity. Their charitable activities were supplementary to the role of civil society in those areas where civil society did not properly perform its role, or they were designed for the immediate relief of misery in the knowledge that it would recur again tomorrow, the cause not having been removed. The later kind of activities involve an attempt to go to the roots of unjust situations whence spring a multitude of evils. The intent is not merely to give solace or to soothe, but to strike at the causes of the trouble.

The growth in awareness of the importance of sociopolitical factors at every level of the human condition has resulted in a shift from an almost exclusive concern with short-term charitable activity, caring for people and consoling them, to an emphasis on long-term concern with the socio-political areas where conditions of life are determined. Religious are to be found there, and lay apostles too, at one with people some of whom espouse an ideology unacceptable to faith, but who also work for a better world. These close contacts and the dialogue which they institute permit them to witness to Christ — to speak to their companions of God's plan for mankind. It is a long road from religious instruction implicit in charitable activity to the harsh reality of discussion of mankind's true nature with work-mates and trade-union officials. But the path is still that of the following of Christ.

One might note in passing that if religious congregations paid little heed in the past to the long-term and were not much concerned with attacking the social sources of evil, it was not because they believed that this conflicted with their vocation. The entire Church, from the laity to the head, did not think of it. And not only the Church! Evolving in unison with society as a whole, the Church for a long time conceived of the fight against misery, to which she was committed, as help to the deprived — for this was how secular agencies did it. The pioneers of social action began in that way. Without indulging in triumphalism, it is good to recall that religious, inspired by their vow of poverty, played an important part in enterprises which gave flesh and blood to the notion of a world in which "justice and peace reign".

## INVOLVEMENT OF RELIGIOUS

Religious no longer wonder whether or not they should become involved in the world of work in a new way. Their practice has already decided the issue. We have already shown what, deep down, has motivated them.

Many of them however ask questions about the *manner* of their involvement. For it is obvious that it is all very tentative. It is a difficult problem, without doubt one of the most complex to face the religious life in the course of its long history. It would indeed be tragic if the present trend towards a presence at the heart of the human ferment were to cause religious to lose their identity. They would have become unfaithful to Christ, who invited them to follow Him, and to the Holy Spirit who sent them to the places where humanity labors. It is a matter of concern to them.

The problem is all the more complex in that in a sense it comprises two questions about the manner of involvement. Both require serious reflection if congregations are to avoid committing their members irrevocably to fruitless endeavors:

> *How* is one to take on new tasks, going about them in new ways, if one intends to do this as a Christian?

> *How* is one as a Christian to take on new tasks, in new ways, if one intends to do this without detriment to the specific characteristics of one's religious institute?

The reply to each of these questions is more difficult than might at first appear.

## Solidarity with the Workers

Let us begin with an assertion. From the viewpoint which we have outlined, there is much more to taking up a secular job than choosing work which is honest, will provide a livelihood, and will contribute to the betterment of society. For it brings with it — and this is usually explicitly envisaged from the beginning — the acceptance of solidarity with the world of work. But, with stern logic, this leads to participation in socio-political movements and organizations (such as trade unions) which channel and shape those desires for emancipation or liberation of which *Evangelii Nuntiandi* speaks. It cannot be denied that, at times to the detriment of objective analysis of situations, these movements and organizations invest such desires with passion and dramatize them. There is an implicit Manicheism which impels one, for example, to divide people into good and bad, as into two clearly distinct categories, solely on the basis of their positions on the social scale, or which refuses to countenance any criticisms of one's position by the other side. It is essential, therefore, when one speaks of the involvement of religious in the world of work, that a clear distinction is made between the job as such (with its objective contribution to the constructive work of the world) and the situation of the worker, with the tight network of solidarity, confrontation aggression and hope which totally circumscribe it. To say nowadays that a religious has become involved in the world of work is by implication to affirm that he has accepted solidarity with the workers. Further, it is to suggest that this solidarity will be more normative and will be more important than the trade or profession itself.

## An Evangelical Vision of Mankind

We have said earlier that in performing a secular task *before* God, one is obeying His will for the transformation of the world. It must now be added that the human situation is by far the most important area for transformation. The post-conciliar Church is convinced that Christians must play their part, in their own measure and in accordance with their calling, in those movements which fight for respect for the person and for justice. For the Church, it is clear that justice means infinitely more than the equitable division of material goods; it involves a "justice of liberty" and a "justice of thought". It is clear that believers must be possessed of a certain vision of the human person — that which tradition draws from Revelation. There are two characteristic elements in this vision.

The first of these key elements has to do with human destiny, conceived not in terms of reward.and punishment, but rather in terms of the complete fulfilmènt, or the failure thereof, of mankind and the universe. Human beings cannot be fully themselves, individually and collectively, except by recognizing their God and entering into a free relationship of friendship with Him. So the Bible tells us. Far from being secondary or from being an extrinsic addition to the mystery of mankind, the relationship to God is at its very center.

The eternal life of which the Creed and the liturgical texts speak is not, then, for Christians an appendix to their efforts to form their lives and their universe. It is the shaping force of the true human destiny. Christians who are involved in the world of work (with its vigorous calls for social justice and for the equitable distribution of wealth) or who labour for the advancement of people, cannot limit their vision to purely temporal choices, equating their lives purely and simply with their struggles for justice and a general material welfare. They place all this in a much bolder horizon.

If the first element of the evangelical understanding of the human person emphasizes the grandeur of those whom God has created "in His image and likeness", the second element emphasizes rather the weakness of the human condition. It is a realistic vision and has little in common with the views of Jean-Jacques Rousseau on the natural goodness of the human person. Revelation never ceases to dwell on the radical fragility of mankind, marred by a native weakness to sin, which leads men and women to succumb to the deep-seated egoism that exists in the human person. It empha-sizes also the inevitable personal and collective encounter between humanity and the drama of evil. And it refuses to minimize the importance of death.

It is well to recall here the great eschatological hope, with its apocalyptic overtones, which runs right through the Bible: during historical time, until the second coming of the Lord, the future can never exhibit the features of a terres-trial paradise. Waves of human weakness and of evil will batter constantly against the dykes erected to safeguard justice, dignity and liberty; little by little they will wear them away. The problem of humanity and of its history can never be reduced to its mere social, economic and political dimen-sions. Christians know — and they do not need a taste of some Gulag to dim their hopes — that even when social justice reigns on earth much will remain to be achieved. Not only must people's minds be opened again to hope of an after-life, but such is the corruption of the human heart that new evils will inevitably be born. The person, which counts for more than any economic values, will be wounded thereby. Revelation, which is nothing if not realistic, urges the believer to a constant and vigilant mobilization of energies on behalf of the dignity and the destiny of the person. And while it may be necessary, especially nowadays, to concentrate most of one's strength on that effort, the struggle is not limited to the socio-economic front. For a Christian, liberty is too profound a reality to be achieved solely by victories won against economic and material alienation. One must act on all fronts. The truly free person is not the person who is simply happy (*heureux*), but the person who is blessed (*bienheureux*), which is something quite different.

### No Cheating About One's Christian Identity

Religious who, with other people, dream of a better world and work to achieve it or seek the betterment of humanity in cultural activities, obviously ought, as Christians, to remain loyal to the Christian vision. They may not cheat about their Christian identity, even if it is not always opportune to reveal it. They cannot disguise their own appearance. This is a matter of honesty towards themselves and towards others — and more fundamentally towards God, *before* whom they act. It obliges them to maintain a critical spirit, in dialogue and in communion with their companions, their organizations and their trade unions. They must even insist on the right to manifest this critical spirit. This is a most important point. Otherwise they will quickly founder in a vague and viscous mixture of Christianity and Marxism and will quite unconsciously end up acting no longer for the Kingdom of God, but for those wholly alien to it. Faced with the intellectual and sentimental intimidation exerted by a seductive ideology, organized and widely publicized throughout society, religious who are sincerely involved in the world of work must strive scrupulously to sharpen their critical spirit and to intensify their intellectual rigour. They can never agree to dismiss the spiritual and mystical dimension of mankind to the margin of society's preoccupations, reducing everything to material and economic questions. For they would be unfaithful to the vision of humanity given in the Scriptures — at once an image of God and a poor sinner, always in need of salvation. Nobody would gain from this, not even the adherents of the ideology in question. Having perhaps recruited one more member, they would have lost the chance of finding themselves questioned, confronted, persuaded to develop.

## To Confess the Name of the Lord

What we have been saying will not wholly satisfy religious who are thinking about the *manner* of their presence in the world of work. Religious have no wish that what has always been characteristic of their way of following Christ should be overshadowed or compromised by their new way of sharing in the mission of God's people. In other words, they want their apostolic activity to remain in perfect harmony with their religious vocation.

Normally of course, this requirement will play a leading role in their choice of work. Their formation and experience, as well as their concern to be faithful to their congregation's vocation, will persuade them to choose a job or profession along the lines envisaged by their founder, or at least in keeping with the spirit of the founder. And if they decide to go in a new direction, they will be careful to choose work which will not be just a way of earning a livelihood, but will be of service to society. This is fully in accord with the secondary purpose of the modern congregations; for the most part they were founded for the practice of charity and of love of humanity. Even if religious decide to take ordinary jobs, like that of an unskilled laborer or a factory worker, unconvinced that what they do is socially useful but "taking what they can get", their work can serve as a means of establishing human contact with other workers and employees and with any people they come across. Earlier, we saw why this is so and there is no point in repeating it. Such ways of acting are sound and they are in harmony with the nature of the religious life.

Although the need for a careful *choice* was not clearly understood at first, nowadays it is accepted that a person's entire religious commitment should be taken into account when choosing an occupation. It seems increasingly abnormal that a religious sister, for example, should look for employment solely in order to earn her living or — as one wrote some ten years ago — "in order to feel appreciated because she too earns a salary". That religious might be forced to become wage-earners in order to provide for their needs —that's understandable. Yet even in such a case, one would expect them at least to *want* to alert their work-mates to their own sense of values. In short, it's difficult to understand how a religious could wish to "work for the sake of working". If religious think it better not to become involved in specific movements of solidarity and association encountered in the working world, they should strive to be at least an evangelical presence calling things in question. Or, in the mystical perspective of the mendicants of the Middle Ages and of Charles de Foucauld in our own era, aspire to enter into secret communion with the mystery of the poor Christ by becoming identified with the most miserably poor. This is profoundly evangelical and in harmony with the following of Christ. Here, however, there comes into play what we would call an almost intrinsic link between the following of Christ (*sequela Christi*) and the need to bear witness in some way, even if it be after a long and patient wait, to the name of the Lord Jesus and of His Father. Even in the most secular occupation, carried on in the most profane context, where there is no immediate possibility of mentioning Christ explicitly, the concern to bear witness and to confess the faith ought to be present. This is a characteristic of the activity of religious and one of their greatest contributions to the mission of God's people.

## The Community

One of the constitutive characteristics of the religious life is its communal dimension. The *koinonia* — of hearts, of wills, of apostolic aspirations, of possessions, of prayer — is essential to it. This *koinonia* stands at the crossing of two coordinates. One of them goes from the individual religious to the community, the other goes from the community as a whole to the individual religious. These two coordinates must be carefully kept in position wherever religious are engaged in rethinking their involvement in the world of work.

The first of these coordinates, that from the individual religious to the community, is the one that nowadays runs the greatest risk of being distorted. It is as well to recall — in order to dispose straightaway of the objection that occurs to many people — that the religious in question are not living outside of obedience, since it is the chapters themselves which have sanctioned their separate involvements in the world of work. It has quite wrongly been suggested, here and there in the Church, that such religious are in fact living outside of obedience. Moreover, it is equally wrong to suggest that when chapters or superiors permit such involvements, they are diminishing the importance of community in religious life. Religious obedience has never — apart from rare exceptions — required that religious should work only as a group, using the same methods, following the same schedules, and doing the same work. Tradition is very strong on this. With regard to the sharing of possessions, the search for the will of God, prayer — in a word, all that can be summed up in the phrase "life-style" — it has rarely been asked of religious that they do all this in common. It is otherwise with classical monastic groups, where the place for community and the place for work are identical, each group forming a small self-sufficient society. The early Dominicans preached in the churches which they found along the way. Each of the early Holy Ghost missionaries settled into his own little corner of wild country. The first Little Sisters of Jesus split up for their work. But such developments are always closely connected with a decision made by the group (or by the authorities speaking in its name), or more or less accepted by it. The obligatory relationship with the community is thus at the very heart of the individual's involvement in this or that milieu.

### Responsibility Towards the Community

Religious who work with their community's approval away from home in secular jobs, with all that this entails, must obviously still be considered part of their community. They are neither exiles in a pagan land, nor are they cast out of the cloister. The fact that they belong to a community is central to their purpose to follow Christ, not alone in an immediate relationship with God and with the Church, but availing themselves of the mediation of a brotherhood or sisterhood. This is provided by their religious family, as formed in a province or, above all, in a community. This mediation is essential to their purpose, whatever concrete form it takes. It is one of the elements which makes each of them truly a religious, and without which they could no longer call themselves religious in the true sense of the word. It is clear then that their basic responsibility is to the group they *belong to*, outside of which they cease to be religious. Their other responsibilities radiate around this — their solidarity with their work-mates, with the apostolic team-effort, even with political activists. To be a religious is the vocation they have received from the Holy Spirit. Their responsibility before the Spirit recalls them to their responsibility towards their community. They are freely linked to it for the sake of being faithful to Christ and for the sake of their commitment to the service of the Kingdom, which is inseparable from such faithfulness. Other forms of solidarity in which they are involved must have a vital relationship to their solidarity with their community.

Properly understood and properly lived up to, this solidarity cannot be an obstacle to other forms of solidarity. On the contrary, it ought to strengthen them. The problem of the nature of obedience comes into play here. In advance of the desire to mortify one's own will, religious obedience calls for a decision that God's will for one's life and its commitment will never be sought for alone — always in company with others. The opportunity offered in baptism will be taken in all seriousness: never again to stand alone, shut fast within the bounds of personal desire and the narrowness of one's own opinions — but to break through one's limitations and enlarge one's vision with the help of one's brothers and sisters. This remains true even when the will of God must be sought for in the difficult situations that arise when one is engaged in a secular occupation — whereof the members of one's community may know little or nothing. It's true that the final decision in most such cases will have to be made by the individual religious, since he or she will be the only person fully competent to make it. Yet in so doing, religious will remain open to what the members of their community put before them, their criticisms, their arguments. This would be impossible if they were unwilling to discuss their activities and their decisions with the community.

There is also the other side to obedience. Fraternal solidarity calls for giving as well as receiving. All religious put themselves at the service of the members of their community to help them expand the limits of their own desires and thus discover the will of the Father.

Religious working outside their community on an absorbing and highly specialised job ought not on that account to exempt themselves from this fraternal service, which is a test of their sincerity as religious. It may also serve as preparation for a further test that may one day face them, when they may have to consider withdrawing from a project which would cement their ties with the workers but which would irrevocably damage their links with their community — a community, let's say, which fails as yet to understand the evangelical character of the project. It is by attitudes like this that a person's real loyalty to the religious life is disclosed. To these must be added a faithful sharing of salaries and other money received. The attraction of ownership being what it is, this is a constant test of solidarity on every level.

## *The Responsibility of the Community*

To speak of community solidarity brings up the other coordinate of *koinonia*, the responsibility of the community towards each member. For if religious who are engaged in a fight for justice and for human rights in a working milieu ought not on that account to cut themselves off from the community to which they belong, the community itself ought not to absolve itself from full responsibility for them. The community is tied to each individual religious when accepted at profession; it is committed to be their support in their struggle to be faithful to their vocation. It must therefore decide to be at one with them in what they do, even if what an individual religious is doing is beyond the competence of the community. The community must see itself as the milieu, the evangelical cell where, thanks to prayer and fraternal love, the individual religious will be supported, enlightened, comforted. It would be hateful and evangelically scandalous if the group as such were to expel a member whose secular job or socio-political opinions were not to its liking.

It is true that the attitude of individual religious under pressure of demands put forward by their co-workers, their colleagues, or the organizations in which they struggle, can often be far from the mentality and the preoccupations of their co-religious. Sometimes the attitude of an individual religious contradicts what another member of the same community has proclaimed publicly, in opting for the other side or another viewpoint. Religious may, for example, support the lay nurses whose rights have been infringed in a hospital run by the congregation to which they belong.

It would be wrong for a community to fragment in the face of this pluralism of positions adopted by members engaged in social action. It is here that the role of the superior or the person responsible takes on its full meaning, for it will be for the superior to foster in the group the realisation that their unity is not rooted in their work in all its variety, but in the call of the Lord. When a community lives a healthy and realistic pluralism, the effect of the challenges, the confrontations, the arguments, the divergence of viewpoints is to lead individual religious to qualify and even to question their own hitherto intransigent viewpoints. Is it necessary to point out that a life in *koinonia* conducted in this fashion is not a sentimental quest for fraternal love? It is, rather, a firm, adult acceptance of responsibility by all for each, with his or her problems. An acceptance of responsibility which each refuses to relinquish. The seriousness of a religious community is judged in the light of this determination.

## A New Face for Community Life

If our prescriptions for ensuring the quality of new forms of involvement in the world of work are to result in something more than wishes and words, it is obvious that congregations of every sort must try to give a new face to their community life. This will be one of the most urgent needs in the coming years. Formalized communities, with starched, stereotyped, interpersonal relationships, will be unable to support religious engaged in the sorts of work which are beginning to emerge. The religious would grow away, little by little, and one day would find themselves total strangers to their own community.

A climate of fraternal openness must be created, one which will enable religious in spite of everything to see themselves as people welded together in a community by the same call *before* God. This would appear to be a *sine qua non* for the success of the new forms of involvement. Left on their own or regarded as free agents, religious will never be able to couple their vocation to follow Christ with their involvement in the increasingly complex human problems which they will encounter. If communities are content to be no more than dormitories to which people return for a little rest, or oratories for the recitation of psalms in common, they might as well shut their doors. They will have killed their future.

On the other hand, it would be wrong to conceive of religious houses as nests of unreal spiritual warmth, havens of psychological and pious satisfaction. One would be speedily deceived. What is needed is to restore the web of unity, taking into account the fact that religious no longer live the entire day under the same roof, are no longer all present at the same community exercises, no longer live their daily lives at the same rhythm, no longer share the same political and social views — at the same time accepting that there is need to fashion a common heart and a common soul, for the sake of Christ and of his call. We are not at the end of our afflictions.

The interventions of superiors, in consequence, must take on new forms at all levels. By a kind of analogical extension of the principle of subsidiarity, it must doubtless come to pass that religious, supported as we have said by community solidarity, will be left to act on their own responsibility where they show themselves capable of seeing clearly by themselves where their responsibility lies. On the other hand, superiors will have to be prepared to supply all the help such people need when they stampede, lose courage, meet a crisis. *Accompaniment*, spiritual and fraternal, takes precedence over *commandment*, even when this is exercised in the milder and more profoundly evangelical manner we have known in the past decade. The authorities in all congregations must do all in their power to ensure in their communities the quality of acceptance, of dialogue and of fraternity of which we have been speaking. If they do this seriously they will restore to their function a lustre which they had thought lost for evermore. For them too, then, a new task.

# CHAPTER II

# The Challenge of Faith

On rereading Pere Lebret's little book *Principes pour l'action*, I came across some lines which made a deep impression on me when I was a young Dominican:

> Set off. You do not know what ships you will meet, what storms will cross your path, what ports you will visit. You will leave, without knowing all that is going to happen, and you will arrive. It is enough that the boat is not leaking, that the holds are full enough, the engines working, and the captain and crew capable of doing their job. There is a risk, but that does not stop you from setting out. (L. J. Lebret, *Principes pour l'action*, L'Abresle, 1944, p. 19).

And further on, before he presents what he calls the principles of permanent revolution "always in advance of any other revolutionary movement" and whose principles he finds in the Gospel, he gives the following instructions to priests in charge of sailors:

> Love them in order to give them an awareness of their
> destiny, so that they will appreciate their value as men
> called by God to the highest form of knowledge, and so
> that they will appreciate God with his proper value as
> God. (*Ibid.*, p. 99).

These two quotations give a fair idea of my present topic.
I shall not argue for a faith which is set at risk to the point
where it is faith no longer. Or for a faith which trifles with
the absolute certainty that God, in Jesus Christ, has spoken,
once and for all, the Word that seals His covenant with
mankind. Or a faith which refuses to admit that it is bound
up with certain basic truths which can in no way be dismissed or even altered, no matter if at times some of its
demands appear excessive. With all my heart, I believe that
faith is so linked with certain fixed and essential principles
that, without them, it can have neither consistency nor any
reason for being. I do feel, however, that this faith must find
expression in action, facing up to practical situations wherein it springs to life. I shall try, therefore, to speak of it in its
"live" aspects, as a living faith for today; for a truly evangelical faith neglects neither the absolutes nor contact with life.


## 1. Faith Today

When you try to study faith in action in today's world,
your first impression may well be that it entails too much
risk. Your reaction will probably be one of puzzlement and
indeed anxiety. Can it be indeed true that the "in the world"
mentality has begun to nibble away slowly at the essentials
of the faith, and with the complicity of some of the most
fervent of the faithful? To use the strong expression of a
novelist, is not the world in the process of "colonizing the
faith by imposing on it its own categories, its visions and its
customs?" One group of Christians is presently making out
a case for this point of view as against the rest of us and the
question is too serious to be ignored.

May I be permitted to take the part of a devil's advocate at this point — reminding you that, although the devil's advocate seldom wins during a process of canonization, he helps enormously to clarify issues. For he puts his finger on those points where real problems exist. He forces people to examine them objectively, and allows no sympathetic feelings to prejudice him or cloud his judgment.

Here begins the devil's advocate's case.

## EROSION OF FAITH

It is a fact that committed Christians, religious men and women moved by a fervent missionary spirit, feel themselves called to witness to the Gospel in the full face of the world. The "place" wherein they must thereafter try to live out their faith identifies, more or less, with human working situations which have for a long time been affected by forces destructive of hope and having often little to do with the faith. For them, as for a large number of Christians from every Church, evangelical witness will be carried out in a place in which the promotion of justice and socio-economic liberation is a prime necessity. These committed Christians find themselves, therefore, with their faith and in its name battered on all sides by powerful currents of opinion which are incident to their new work surroundings. The result may well be a deepening of faith, but it could also be the slow erosion of faith — or, at least, a growing uncertainty about the bases on which faith rests. It is important to stress clearly at this point the many ways in which faith runs the risk of disintegration in such a context.

### Wanting to be "Relevant"

The first of these ways, and a principal one, results from what we may call the desire to be relevant. This is a new word in the missionary vocabulary which seeks to emphasize that there is a necessary bond between the Gospel and the possibility of modern man accepting it. If it is to be "relevant" (so it is said), the Gospel message must fit into human situations so that it is seen to make common cause with them and answer their questions. It will be welcomed — and faith thereby firmly rooted — to the degree that shows itself relevant. Indeed, if you want the Gospel to "catch on" today, you must present it in such a way that the individual men and women to whom you are preaching find that it expresses their own deepest concerns and deals with them — that it is in line with their own everyday needs and desires.

Here we have a problem. In apostolic work, such insistence that faith be relevant can result in an unintentional relativizing, minimizing, even total neglect of certain elements which are at the heart of the Christian identity. Because they have little in common with modern ideas, or seem opposed to most of the aspirations that our contemporaries affect, these elementary truths are no longer stressed. Admittedly, there is a hierarchy among the truths of the faith and not all are of equal importance, so I shall limit myself to showing how some of the points which are central to faith are being neglected.

It is evident that no Christian who is truly committed to the Gospel could accept the disappearance of the figure of Jesus Christ from the field of his apostolic consciousness. Yet it must be admitted that sometimes, for the sake of appearing "relevant", some of the most distinctive characteristics of the mystery of Jesus are down-played.

Without any doubt, the greatest temptation along these lines is to make Christ a moral system, to look on Him as a message and not someone who reveals God. While it is clear that, for the Scriptures, the decisive contribution of Jesus "was to show in the life of a man like us" the face of God, nowadays people prefer to present Him as somebody who challenges one to a commitment, to question accepted values: — who galvanizes one into activity, while no attention is paid to the essential link which unites Him to God. As the Reverend A. Dumas truly remarks, at times one may almost approach a sort of christological atheism, God becoming a myth in proportion as Jesus becomes a message, and the obvious attraction of Jesus dispensing one from having to consider God to whom Jesus should lead. It is also remarkable that "our age is becoming less and less certain of God, as it gets more interested in examining the historicity of Jesus." People are interested in Jesus especially as a human model, someone who challenges one's conscience, someone who preaches a message which shakes the world. Does this kind of concentration on Jesus take account of everything at the heart of evangelical faith? Cut off from his explicit relationship with the mystery of God, is Jesus still Christ?

Now it can happen that what began as an attempt to understand, a starting point from which to develop a fuller presentation of the faith, can change bit by bit into a question and then a personal conviction. Committed Christians, religious men and women, who are sincere and upright end up by asking themselves whether what does not "work," what does not "catch on," has any meaning. The reservations of contemporary society become one's own reservations. From the question "How should one speak about Christ?" one slips unawares to the question "Who really is Jesus Christ?" if we take as the framework of our reading and understanding the way in which contemporary society reacts against the specific teaching of the Gospel. At the very bottom of a courageous commitment to the Gospel, the *in the world* quality may well be destroying faith.

### Faith a Luxury?

This leads us to the second source of *erosion* of the faith through a present-day commitment to working in modern society. Usually the most committed Christians, religious or lay, have become thus committed, or have become involved in such work, principally in order to serve others in the name of the Gospel, and this is often seen as more important to them than the witness given to the Gospel. Acquaintance, and friendship too, with unbelievers who are engaged in the same tasks and show just as much devotedness and hard work, give rise to questions like: "What precisely does my faith add to my commitment?" "To what extent am I working *for the sake of* my faith?" Surely, after working for several years in a human situation, will not their principal motivation become one or other social need, which has no necessary link with the faith we have been considering? Even if these Christians do not ask themselves this question, it is inevitable that unbelievers will do so.

To give an honest answer to this question it is not enough to call on the name of Jesus; one has to plumb the depths of the mystery of Jesus, which is quite a different thing. Many people feel quite lost when faced with this task. Traditional modes of thought seem useless to answer their questionings, and cynics upset them even more with their ever-ready suspicions whose objective value few are capable of judging. Naturally, it is tempting to look for a solution, or at least a provisional one, by reducing the mystery of Jesus Christ to its ethical dimensions, as I have described. But few Christians will be satisfied with this. Whenever the inevitable question about what is specific in faith finds no certain answer, and especially when a person has strong motivation in a commitment to social needs, another question quickly presents itself: "Why am I still a Christian?" This is all the more so, let me repeat, because the social needs of people has very often been the determining element in the choice of commitment.

In the event that one's commitment to the social needs of people no longer seems to need Christianity to justify it, or give it new drive, it is only normal that one should wonder if faith is not superfluous. This feeling increases when the faith separates one, apparently without reason, from non-Christian fellow-workers. Is faith just a luxury then? The resulting sense of unease becomes all the more painful when the Church declares officially that there is a radical incompatibility between the faith and an interpretation of facts which concrete experience seems to oblige one to accept.

This does not necessarily oblige anyone to give up the faith. In spite of all, prayer can help one fight to save one's faith. However, upsetting questions continue to torment the conscience:

Is my being a Christian just something left over from my past, which I have not the courage to leave behind me? Am I a Christian simply because I am afraid not to be, afraid of being nothing? And, especially if I am a priest or a religious, and if I realize that an interior change of this kind, honestly faced up to, would have enormous implications in my social and professional life." (G. Girardi, *Nouveaut chrétienne et nouveaut de monde*)

It should be noted that it is not the color of opinion, or its extremism either to left or right, that matters, but the link between this commitment and the faith. Generosity in the service of others, which in the vast majority of cases is the deepest motive for action and the most radical source of commitment, may become detached from the faith. But when faith ceases to have any influence on action, it is useless, like a tawdry ornament.

## To Be Where the Action Is

And now we come to another way in which faith is being weakened. This time it is by an automatic sympathy for everything which plays a positive part in human society. This is seen in the desire to be *with it* — to share those efforts which try to produce a new person or a new society. Reacting against a not too distant past when a Christian was expected to be suspicious of everything new in the profane world, the modern committed believer instinctively feels one that should be open and welcoming to new ideas.

Now, it is always difficult to have clear ideas about movements which aim to change society. Once again generosity is not enough; it must be enlightened. Christians must of necessity compare with their faith any idea which they are asked to accept or condemn, and this is often a delicate process in which it is impossible to come to any definite conclusion. Who can make black and white distinctions, on the basis of the Gospel, between the violence used by one social class against another, and the violence used by liberation movements looking for a more just society? On the other hand, who can determine the precise moment when demands in favour of an oppressed social class seeking for justice become unjust for another class, reversing the situation but doing nothing to stop the injustice? Is it possible to put one's finger on the exact link between rejecting one or other political programme and being unfaithful to the evangelical call to love the poor and the weak? The faith gives no clear answer, and this lack of direction seems to be an obstacle to people who are making a generous effort to play their part in those movements which are trying to change society and prepare for the future. It is only a short step from that to the notion that faith automatically leads to conservatism, and that when all is said and done, "life would be easier without it." Commitment to modern society and the solidarity one feels with it, in a word, the *in the world* quality implied in being a committed Christian, runs the risk of weakening and then blotting out the very demands of faith itself.

And here ends the case for the devil's advocate.

## *What is True in These Objections?*

Nobody will deny that there is a certain amount of truth in the foregoing objections. To refuse to admit this would be foolish, and tantamount to a refusal to consider evidence and to a stubborn insistence that one's own position measures up exactly to the faith and is an infallible guide to the message of the Gospel. The devil's advocate case, as I have stated it, represents an extreme condition of affairs. In a normal situation, as we are all aware, many qualifications would obtain. What the devil's advocate says is almost a caricature. Like all good caricatures, however, by stripping its subject of subtleties and shadings it represents the characteristic ideas of our times in their starkest form. Its very exaggerations serve to sharpen the outline.

Let us be honest with ourselves. Is there any committed Christian, lay or religious, working in modern situations, who has not at times said to himself or herself that their commitment could end up in just such a manner? Does not every Bishop, Superior General, or Provincial wonder anxiously at times if some community, or group, or worker, or priest, or religious has not gone beyond the point of no return in this regard? What I have exaggerated and caricatured brings out an element of Christian commitment today which is a threat of evil, if not its actual presence — a something which is a profound worry to the Christian conscience. It would be unpardonably flippant and foolish simply to dismiss all this concern by labeling it "conservative" and "hide-bound." The devil's advocate is only saying out loud what every one of us whispers to himself or herself at one time or another, ashamed perhaps of saying it but relieved all the same for having done so. He is putting into words what theology calls the *sensus fidelium*. And this *sensus fidelium* speaks to the churches in a still, small voice: "This is how committed Christians who generously set themselves to work *in the world* for the Gospel's sake may end up...if their worldly activity is not held in the right direction by another essential element of the Christian mystery."

That "if", which the devil's advocate did not consider, is just as important as his case because it puts it into perspective. It alters everything and brightens the horizon considerably. Being *in the world* no longer seems something needful which one should attempt, but only with great care and many precautions; rather, it is seen as something essential which is full of risk. Quite a different thing.

## "IN THE WORLD" — RISKY BUT ESSENTIAL

Being *in the world* is an essential element of the faith, to the extent that without it faith would no longer be a living thing. During this era between Easter and the Parousia, the world, for the follower of Christ is not just a sort of container, a geographical and historical envelope upon which one can look with indifference simply because it is on the outside. Because it implies a covenant with Christ, the Lord of history, if faith is to be real, it must take flesh in history.

We must be careful here of a too simplistic use of certain texts of the New Testament, dating from the time when the

first Christians lived in the expectation of an immediate
return of Christ. When it was understood that the Parousia
was not to come immediately, ideas changed about the
Christian attitude to the link between the service of Christ
and one's own presence in history of which He is the Lord
until that day "when he hands over the kingdom to God the
Father, having put all his enemies under his feet" (1 Cor
15:24). Indeed when tradition speaks about living in a historical period, it means something other than a benevolent
presence, or that we should remain untouched among the
waves, like a granite reef wearing on its crown an age-old
lighthouse. It even means something more than being a
missionary and simply going off to spread the Good News,
passing on the truth as a master passes on teaching. Faith
enters into history when it allows itself to be affected by the
situations it faces up to and the contexts in which it works;
faith becomes part of history when it takes to itself what is
human, just as a river envelops ice. This process is not
simply a matter of passing on an abstract truth from one
milieu to another, one generation to another — just as the
ideas of Plato or Hegel might be passed on — but (to use the
johannine expression) by *making* this truth. Living faith
implies bringing evangelical truth to birth just as much as
keeping intact truth already accepted. It demands a continual expression in action of faith already received. It means
complete loyalty to the Credo of the Fathers, in osmosis
with life which is always in a condition of renewal. This is
the very essence of tradition. Contrary to what "traditional-
ists" of all sorts may think, tradition implies openness and
development as much as fidelity to the past.

### Relevance: A Constituent of Living Faith

Bearing all this in mind, the question of relevance can be
properly understood. It will no longer be seen simply as a
teaching process, still less as a makeshift device which must
be accepted on account of the difficult times we live in. On
the contrary, it will be seen to be a constituent part of living
faith, necessary for its interaction with history. It is impor-

tant to remember that ever since Paul met the Gentiles, ever since the heated discussion at the Council of Jerusalem (Acts 15:2-7) on Jewish observances, Christian faith has continually had to deal with questions, sometimes put in a violent way, coming to it from the world. The atmosphere which surrounded the Councils of Nicea and Chaldedon was one of searching for the relevance of the faith in the world of Greek culture. And who can deny that the *in the world* quality has left its mark on the most precious and solemn formulas of Christianity, those which try to describe the mystery of the person of the Lord Jesus Christ? And it was the same with the ideas that came to the surface at the time of the Reformation, when European culture was beginning a new phase. Faith will only endure when it is challenged, when it is affected by the great questions of the day, the problems and anxieties of the moment. It follows that the answers faith makes to these questions will have a strong effect on the way faith expresses itself. Conceived of and held, not abstractly as in a collection of dogmas or a treatise on beliefs, but (as we are doing here) as a living thing, faith rarely shows the balance of a treatise or a collection of dogmas. It lives all the time with qualifications. This does not imply that it betrays its principles. Rather does it mean that faith tries to be relevant, to be what it should be: God's call made, not to humanity at large, but to individual men and women of flesh and blood tossed about by the aims, the ideals, the virtues and the vices of their age.

Now it is clear that our time in the present state of the world, has to face up to difficult problems which are lumped together under the often ambiguous label of human advancement, liberation, transformation of society. By criticizing realistically the socio-economic conditions of a large section of humanity, whom they have led rather successfully to appreciate the reasons for their present state, Marxists have created a state of mind, a mood of expectation. As N. Berdiaeff has aptly pointed out, they have also set up a new messianism, with its emphasis on a liberating *praxis*, urging people to strive for a state of social justice. This happened just at the time when the churches were paying little atten-

tion to the earthly side of the Gospel. This is the slant that
our present day world puts on its questions to the faith, and
with no apologies either. Is not the faith messianic? Does
not the faith proclaim that Jesus, the Son of God, is Christ
and Messiah? Does it not declare that the Church, the group
of those who believe, is a messianic people? Equally in this
spirit, the world offers itself to the faith as the place where it
must work, where it must be seen to be relevant. It will
become a living faith incarnate in the world, serving the
Lordship of Christ and involved in the life of the world, by
making an effort to "catch up" and thus renew in itself its
messianic role.

The problems we face today therefore are neither artificial nor unusual. And the way in which the churches are
trying to put into action the *in the world* quality of their
faith, far from being a betrayal of faith, serves rather to
highlight one of its essential components — that which
allows it to take its part in the life of the world, to plant there
the seed of the Kingdom, and renew itself in the process. The
intense commitment it shows in its efforts to bring about a
new humanity is by no means a rejection of its true Christian
responsibilities, or the extinction of the spirit of the Gospel.
On the contrary it is no less than the beating of the Church's
heart in the body of the world, which to the last day of
history, is and will remain its own. For the Church is only
the Body of Christ *in the world*, the everyday world described in the newspapers, the world of work and recreation,
of tears of distress and of joy, of hands stretched out for war
or peace, the world of old people and young, those from
under-developed countries as for those who are dying from
over-eating and over-drinking, those who believe and those
who have no faith. To refuse to play its part there, would be
for the Church to refuse to have a living faith. And that
would be a betrayal.

## The World Fertilized by the Gospel

It would also be a refusal to be evangelical in both senses
of the word, because to evangelize does not simply mean to

announce the Gospel, to preach the Good News in all parts
of the world. It also means to fertilize the world with the
Gospel so that people may become what the Gospel wants
them to be; and this even if the name of Jesus is never
spoken, because people are not prepared enough to accept
it. For before it is a reality that can be spread abroad, the
Kingdom must be brought into being as a reality. Besides to
evangelize is not simply thus to change the world in line with
the Gospel. It also means to feel intensely worried about the
"future of the faith" and to seek to spread the faith in such a
way that, on the one hand, to the end of time the evangelical
leaven will not cease to be mixed in with human society to
make visible there the-mankind-that-God-wills, and that on
the other hand, the name of the Lord Jesus will continue to
be adored and glorified in it. The Kingdom comprises the
whole of history, and the two elements are inseparably
linked. Faith will more easily be spread by the authentic way
in which it is lived than by the way in which it is taught and
preached. Witness makes words blossom, and this has been
the way since the beginning:

> I suppose there always have been people especially
> consecrated to missionary work, and particularly in pla-
> ces where the native culture offered greater resistance to
> acceptance of the faith. But the Churches of those times
> (the first centuries of Christianity) do not seem to have
> been preoccupied with defining and putting into practice
> plans and methods of preaching and propaganda, in spite
> of the pagan masses which surrounded them on all sides.
> "The Word of God continued to spread" by its own
> internal power of attraction, carried far afield by the hope
> which it gave to these same masses, and by the quality of
> its faith and of the life of Christians in their ordinary
> dealings with their neighbours.( L. Moingt, *La transmis-
> sion de la Foi*, Paris, 1976, pp. 51-52.)

Besides, although the writings of Paul and the Acts of the
Apostles stress the sending of missionaries to announce the
Word, those of John show that once the Christian commu-

nities were set up, their witness and the way their lives reflected the hope which was in them on account of the Risen Christ became the principal care of the Church.

Nobody will deny that in our days this witness of Christian communities expresses itself in a commitment to share in movements for the betterment of mankind. Taking part in bringing about necessary changes in society has become one of the major elements in evangelization, and this certainly is a big change. This is a new age in the tradition of the Church, in which the Gospel filters into the world rather through the *humanum*, seen in its sociopolitical dimensions, than through religious searching for God or the desire for mystical experience. In his apostolic exhortation *Evangelii Nuntiandi* of 8th December 1975, Paul VI himself did not hesitate to write the following courageous lines, already quoted:

> There are close links between evangelization and human advancement — development, liberation. Links in the anthropological order because man in need of evangelization is not an abstract being, but one who is subject to social and economic questions. Links in the theological order because one cannot dissociate the plan of creation and the plan of redemption, which latter touches the very concrete situations of injustice to be fought against and justice to be restored. Links of that supremely evangelical order which is charity: for how could the new commandment be proclaimed without promoting in justice and peace the true and authentic growth of mankind?. . . . It is impossible to accept that the work of evangelization could or should neglect those very serious questions, so much in the news today, concerning justice, freedom, development and peace in the world. If that happened it would be to ignore the teaching of the Gospel on the love of one's neighbour who is suffering or in want.

In a perspective limited rather to simply preaching the Gospel, the Bishops' Synod of 1971 had already declared:

This mission to preach the Gospel demands today a
radical commitment to work for the complete freedom of
mankind, now, in the concrete reality of his existence in
this world. If the Christian message of love and justice is
not translated into action for justice in the world, it will
hardly be credible for modern man.

We are dealing here not with a faith that is militant and
out to conquer by reason of some extraordinary charism,
but quite simply with a living faith. The old scholastic
philosophy used to say that faith became alive, i.e. living,
through charity. In our days the "miracle of charity"—for
long the support of evangelization (in the full sense that I
have given to this word, both preaching the Gospel and
bringing it into being)—has taken a new form: commitment
to human problems and sharing in movements that try to
change society. If Christians refused to take their part *in the
world* they would be calling into question the present and
the future of faith in Christ. They would kill the faith
because they would prevent its being accepted by people.
Faith would be just an ephemeral possession of a ghetto, cut
off from life, without any influence on society. Who would
dare to perpetrate such a crime against God and man? Who
could accept that the Name of Jesus would be seen in future
only in the windows of bookshops, where the Gospel was for
sale side by side with the complete works of Aristotle? There
can be no doubt that the fashion in which today's Church
understands its relationship with the world, things being
what they are, is a necessary condition for the existence of
the faith as a living faith. It is what the circumstances
demand.

## Personal Risk. . . Community Risk

This *in the world* quality is a risk, and a great risk. It is a
personal risk for those who are involved in contentious
issues, who are struggling in milieus influenced by alluring
ideologies and who at times feel they find more support and
understanding from non-believing friends than from their

fellow-Christians. It is a collective risk for the faith itself, which is criticized and has to force its way along a slippery track where it could easily get bogged down.

The case made by the devil's advocate, then, made some very pertinent points, and that is why it was necessary to hear it. It made one aware of pitfalls which could catch the unwary or the imprudent. I must repeat that what is at stake is more important than the discomfort or the personal perseverance of the believers in question. We are dealing with the faith itself. In its efforts to "convert" the people and the milieus of our time, the faith must not allow itself to be converted by them. If the Gospel is relevant today because of the commitment of Christians to the great movements of humanity, it cannot for all that permit itself to be destroyed by them. This would be an exercise of masochism, not evangelization.

What is to be done then? We must not remove the faith from the world, looking for a retreat that is more sheltered and more protected. Nor must we put the *in the world* quality, as I have described it, over against the *not of the world* quality, which is the other essential characteristic, without which the faith, however generous, committed and relevant, is no longer a living faith, and so is no longer faith at all.

## 2. *"In the World" and "Not of the World"*

It is just as necessary to pray as to sow in order to reap the harvest, or to use any source whatever of energy to make a machine go. Even in natural things, insofar as they serve mankind, humanity which does not pray can indeed through its science and technology achieve a wonderful control of matter, but if it does not pray, all this will turn out badly for it. Humanity will be the slave of matter instead of using matter for its own liberation, and by breaking the atom mankind will become the slave of dust. (J. Maritain, *Carnet de notes*, Desclée, 1965, p. 388.)

Jacques Maritain is not thinking of prayer that is cut off from commitment to world problems. He describes, rather, *in the world* commitment that is cut off from prayer. The difference is clear. In his somewhat abrupt style, he expresses the fundamental Christian conviction, which throws a great light on the situation in which we find ourselves. While working in the everyday world as we have been considering it up to this point — the world that is formed by human designs and stirred by the forces of change — the Christian does not limit his horizon just to this world. For him the *in the world* quality is intersected by another dimension of the faith, the *not of the world* quality. Called by the Spirit of Christ to live his faith *in the world* by striving to extend in it the power of salvation which would transform humanity into the Kingdom of God, the believer realizes that in the depths of his being he is *not of the world*. In the world...*not of the world*. This is the Christian paradox.

## BEING A CHRISTIAN IN THE LIGHT OF JESUS

It is obvious that the only way out of the difficulty is, once again, to seek to understand what being a Christian is, in the light of the mystery of Jesus. However different they are in their theological interpretations — John does not look on salvation in the same way as Paul; Matthew's idea of the Kingdom is not that of Luke; the Acts of the Apostles presents the spread of the Gospel in a different way from the Johannine texts — the books of the New Testament are unanimous about one point which seems of capital importance to them. God is not present in the person and the work of Jesus simply to put humanity back on the right track by giving to the great motivating forces in history what is necessary to keep them from going astray, or even to redeem the fault which prevents people from becoming good workers in the building of a just society. God also wills to open up a new dimension to the destiny of all humanity, and of each individual person, and to lead human history on to a higher plane, which, left to their own resources, even healed of their defects, human beings could never claim to reach.

And all this in the mystery of a covenant in which the goodness of God uses human responsibility and vocation, not denying them, or putting them aside, or replacing them with other values, but leading them on to excellence in line with what mankind desires and looks for. Properly understood, the Incarnation is this covenant of God and mankind, sprung from God's initiative, but also making use of human responsibility, to lead mankind into what Scripture calls the Kingdom. The *et incarnatus est* thus becomes inseparable from *sedet ad dexteram Patris,* and *in the world* unintelligible without *not of the world.*

## THE QUESTION OF GOD AT THE VERY ROOT OF THE GOSPEL EXPERIENCE

The question of God is at the very root of the Gospel experience and of living faith. Not as an abstract question but as the most important existential question — the one which for a Christian determines once and for all the human vocation and gives life its authentic meaning. One appreciates why it should be central to the worry felt by committed Christians over the relevance of the Gospel. In our irreligious and post-Christian world it is certainly the most difficult question. In Athens Paul could rely on the religious awareness of his hearers to preach hope in Christ to them (Acts 17:16-34); but this is not the case in our Western society. Our contemporaries are no longer pagans, they are post-Christians. They do not consider themselves to be ignorant of Christianity. They believe they have left it behind them, both in the history of their culture and in their personal lives. But for the Christian there can be no getting away from the question of God. It is more fundamental than the problem of *relevance* — whose position in living the faith we have seen — since it gives relevance its point. It is surely not an exaggeration to say that for a believer, once this question is put aside, no other question can have any serious effect on life in the evangelical sense.

Therefore a Christian cannot permit himself or herself to suppress this question at will, since it is deep-set in a Christian and will not go away. To live the faith as a Christian means to live this question; and to live it as the determinant of one's responsibility to the world just as the life and mission of Jesus were shaped and determined by the question of Him whom Jesus called the Father. Leave out of account the question of the Father, and the Gospel no longer exists. A Christian is a person who lives by an answer, difficult at times and often confused by the murmurings of his own difficulties and those of his contemporaries, but ever repeated deep down in his conscience: God has linked himself to mankind, and the fate of history depends above all on this adventure of God with mankind. It is here and here alone that the *et incarnatus est* of Jesus and the *in the world* quality of the Church find their true purpose. Without an awareness of God, Christianity becomes a farce and loses all credibility in the face of the mass ideologies which draw humanity into their service.

## ADORATION — FAITH LIVED IN THE PRESENCE OF GOD

This mutual adventure in which God binds himself in a covenant with mankind is carried out on two different levels which are closely connected. The first of these is the more mysterious but also the more radical. In it is fulfilled what Christianity considers its most precious truth: God wills to share his life with mankind, not just simply as Creator, or even Redeemer, but God-with-mankind. This sharing becomes so real that a son of man, Jesus, is also in the very depths of his being the Son of God. Moreover, the whole New Testament stresses that every person is called to share in some way in this mysterious identity of the Son-of-God-made-man. A mysterious sharing indeed — nonetheless, faith is aware that it is only in this way that God and mankind are seen to be what they really are.

Whenever a Christian becomes conscious of this he feels drawn to give pride of place to adoration among his activities in the world, however down to earth these are. And I repeat, adoration—not prayers and devotions. It is especially important to stress this because on all sides in our Western societies the need for contemplation is beginning to make itself felt and there is a danger that this will be adversely affected and lapse into unbridled religiosity. Working *in the world*, bravely sharing in efforts to bring about liberation — these are truly evangelical if carried out *before God*, and in a spirit of adoration. Otherwise not.

It would be well at this point to return to the case which the devil's advocate made, in order to round it off. If we find ourselves slipping into the frame of mind he describes, it is because we have neglected this need for adoration — perhaps even become suspicious of it — and this because, while we were reflecting over our involvement in the world, we did not allow for a due measure of the contemplative silence in which the faith lives *before God*. We have failed to realize that before it is the origin of the urge to be *relevant* which we find in ourselves, faith is a gift of grace.

The problem of our times is not how much we should become involved *in the world*. No limit can be set to the intensity, whole-heartedness, and realism of our working in the world for the sake of the Gospel, just as there was no limit to the Incarnation of the Son of God who took on a complete human nature, sin alone excepted, even to a descent into hell. Nor can our service ever be too generous, for no limit can be set to generosity shown in the name of the Gospel. Our trouble arises from our becoming involved in the world without adoring God. I have said already that truth is *brought about* by our efforts to answer the questions put to us by the world, and by the quest for relevance which brings truth to birth; but in this process it is adoration — the total recognition of God's gift by heart and mind — which is the nurturing womb without which nothing viable can be born.

We have arrived at a stage when to think of going back to former attitudes concerning the involvement of committed Christians *in the world* of pitiful suffering and noble ideals would be an irreparable mistake and a rejection of the Gospel. It is, however, necessary to reassert the rightful importance of the theological dimension of the life of faith.

In doing this, we must avoid certain clichés which cloud the Gospel vision of a believer's relationship with God and with mankind. In recent times, wordy arguments about the fact that the first great commandment (the love of God) lives only through the second (the love of our fellows), together with noisy claims that contemplation immobilizes action, have contributed largely to the confinement of the life of faith within the strict limits of a life lived morally — and even to the consideration of the faith as just another moral system. It is true that self-giving which at times approaches heroism and uncompromising solidarity with the least of our fellows are great and wonderful things but they too often lack the quickening theological spark which is to be found in the dedication of a Francis of Assisi or a Madeleine Delbrel. There is nothing typically Christian about morality in itself; outside Christianity, you can find just as much commitment, courage, heroism. What is specifically Christian comes from the theological dimension, and from that alone. But what is theological must not be confused with what is devotional or with pietism.

## THE THEOLOGICAL FOUNDATION OF INVOLVEMENT

We are now in a position to locate and make precise the second level at which the adventure of the covenant of God and mankind is carried out. If the true vocation of man is indeed to be brought to share in the life of God, this implies of its very nature a need and a responsibility.

The word *need* should be understood not as an obligation imposed or a necessary condition for earning a reward but as the logical consequence of this communion of God and people. The people of God, apart from making the Name of God known among humanity, must also become, in some sense, God's party in the world. Obviously, this is the party which promotes and defends God's design for humanity, which is none other than the ultimate good of mankind. Therefore it is involved *in the world* so that humanity may become not just what it could be by the correction and strengthening of its own dynamic forces, but the humanity-which-God-wills. For although the full sharing of humanity in the life of God depends on the power of God freely exerted and is quite beyond human efforts, nevertheless it does depend on mankind and especially on Christians whether history between the Resurrection and the Parousia will or will not be open to the Lordship of Christ. In fact, it is precisely by way of human freedom that God intervenes so that humankind may achieve what He has destined for it: the human freedom of Abraham, Jeremiah, Mary, Jesus Christ, Paul, every Christian, every person of good will. But human freedom is such that one can turn against God, so much so that the Fathers of the Church have interpreted mankind's creation as a risk taken deliberately by God. Here then, the Christian perceives himself responsible so to become involved that history, blighted by evil as it is, may despite this develop as God wishes it to develop — mankind playing its true role in the process.

*Before God* then, the Christian is committed to work for the accomplishment of God's plan, and it is to God and not men that he must give an account of this commitment. This he does in the name of his faith, — not because it is a duty laid on him by a Church law, and much less a task which society gives to believers in the name of ordinary human solidarity. The believer's motive is truth itself which flows from his sharing in the life of God, and therefore depends on no command, order or mission. Just as in the union of husband and wife, one exists for the other on account of the very power that binds them together, so the people of God cannot but exist for their Lord and go to the ends of the earth so that God's plan may be fulfilled.

Why become involved in the world then? Why try to approach, not the threshold of the problems and hopes of humanity, but their very hearth, ready to be burnt in the process? On account of God and of what Jesus Christ is for the believer, not principally or fundamentally on account of human solidarity. The *not of the world* quality is the driving force of the *in the world* quality, though it imposes no other limit on *in the world* than acceptance of God's will for the world. "God so loved the world that He gave His only Son. . . " (John 3:16) and His Spirit continues to send His adopted sons into the world.

Having its roots in a familiarity with God, and not first and foremost in human solidarity, is what gives to Christian involvement its special character and shape. The standard which , in the last analysis and when all is said and done, has to be measured up to, is to be found in God (as he reveals himself in Jesus Christ) and not in the call of the world. And if you search the Gospels for the rule to follow, you must be careful not to read them with worldly eyes or in the light of strained and fanciful interpretations. This has always been disastrous for those who are ignorant of the theological roots of Christian involvement *in the world*. For committed Christians sharing a human situation with which they feel deep solidarity, it can be crucifying — the more so in that the Gospel has quite a different system of values from those of our world. Above all it refuses to look on any other person as an enemy, and preaches love and good will to all others, a love which is disinterested to the point of taking the risk that love will not be returned. It even claims that it is only this love that will produce in this world the humanity-that-God-wants.

## THE STATUS OF LIVING FAITH

The johannine formula *in the world — not of the world* is, consequently, no vague formula of spirituality. Indeed, better perhaps than in other periods, does it express today the status of living faith. Unless it plays its part *in the world* and in its striving, the faith is not involved; it loses its relevance and even runs the risk of fading away in the future. Converted to the world, however, to the extent of becoming one with its values and aims in an uncritical fashion, the faith loses its character. What is lived and passed along thus may well be a noble and generous human experience, but it is no longer the faith. There is no living faith without continuing tension between *in the world* and *not of the world*. Naturally this tension can only exist when one refuses to suppress or seriously weaken either of these.

How strikingly N. Berdiaeff puts this in his lucid analysis of the relationship between Christianity and Marxism:

> All utopias... must be judged by what is absolute in Christianity, but one can by no means conclude from this that Christians need not bother about the struggle that is going on in the world. More than this, they must make up their minds to take a part in this struggle.... History is accomplished by God and by man. For history must not be understood to be simply a human perfection or a divine perfection, but rather a reality in which God and man play their part. Humanity has a part in the human nature of Christ.... It is only by starting from this fact that history can be understood. It must be seen as part of a human-divine process, a tragic cooperation of God and man. (*Christianisme Marxisme*, pp. 34-35)

*

What has been said here about the need to make the faith come alive in socio-political action is also true of that other essential responsibility of the Christian community — handing on the faith. Unless the faith is handed on, expressed in a relevant way but unchanged in its content, "in twenty years time, young people will go, like archaeologists, to examine its dead and dusty texts in ruins and libraries." The text of the major articles of the creed cannot be changed, even if it is found to be upsetting. Otherwise one would not be handing on the faith of the Gospel but an artificial entity based on the ideas and ideologies of the moment, in line with the passing fashions of the world. Neither is it right to pass lightly over what is found to be embarrassing and out of favour today. The faith by its very nature and its purpose can be communicated, but it must be expressed in intelligible human terms if it is to be grasped. Faith is quite pointless if it has no message; it is irrelevant if it has lost the power to deliver this message. In a word, faith can only live where there is a tension between communion with the world and its needs and searching, and, on the other hand, the refusal to set aside the deepest reasons for believing. One cannot take refuge in vague and woolly notions of God, or think of the Christian faith as the witness to an unforgettable man, a remarkable man, eternally imprinted on the collective memory of mankind, and who is called Jesus Christ, and nothing more than this.

## The Mystery of Jesus

In the dogmatic perspective, this tension of *in the world* and *not of the world* sums up the mystery of Jesus. It is well known that the great doctrinal schisms which shook the faith of the Church during the first centuries took their origins precisely in the temptation to remove one or the other of these principles. The Christ whom we serve cannot be separated from Jesus of the Incarnation, "a man like us in all things but sin," Who has entered into the glory of God and so possesses the Name which is above all names. He is alive today in the tension between *in the world* and *not of the world*. Not just man, not just God, but the mysterious meeting of the truth of man and the truth of God. Now between Easter and the Parousia the life of faith is the witness to Christ made manifest in His Body, the Church. This reflects and in a way perpetuates the clash which gives the Christian event its nature: the meeting between complete involvement with the world of mankind, and total belonging to the world of God. Like Christ, whom the faith believes to be not one *or* the other but one *and* the other, so also faith which remains living insofar as it keeps alive the tension between *not of the world* but still *in the world, in the world* but still *not of the world*.

I have used the term tension, and I do not mean equilibrium. The more one studies the history of living tradition the more one becomes aware that a perfect equilibrium between *in the world* and *not of the world* is not only rarely found but that it is hard to say what it really consists in. This is the price one pays for living. Against fundamentalism of all sorts which preaches a dead conformity of the present with the past, the Catholic vision has never ceased insisting on the idea of a living tradition. In ecumenical dialogue, this surely is one of the most important points which Catholics try to present to their brothers and sisters of other Christian confessions. Faith lives continually on a tight rope. As soon as one has regained balance for an instant one begins to lean again to left or right. The essential is to keep on going and not to decide, either because one gets tired or loses faith, to come down from the tight rope. Let's look at history — at what preceded the Council of Nicea under the influence of the teaching of Arius, and then what came before Chalcedon in the wake of Eutyches' ideas; at the thomistic notion of grace with its strong emphasis on God who justified, and the ideas of the theologians of the Society of Jesus stressing rather the role of mankind; at the preference of the Church for the contemplative life and then at a great insistence on apostolic involvement; at a stress on the supernatural mission of the People of God followed by a vigorous reminder of its responsibility in history. At the end of his little book *Initiation á la priére* Romano Guardini, probably inspired by Bergson, wrote, "What is alive, moves." This applies to faith, too. What is required is that it never cease to move between its two coordinates *in the world* and *not of the world*, and that it never leave either of them aside.

## A Clash of Attitudes

If we do not take care, and especially if we do not properly understand the law of life which the tension I have described represents for the faith, it is possible that exclusive polarizations will come about, putting at risk the unity of the Christian community and the future of the faith. Indeed it is possible to see signs of this in certain movements that are developing today.

On the one hand, a growing number of people who find in modern forms of evangelization too much sinking of differences between Christianity and popular ideologies are standing aloof and clamoring for a "return to the spiritual." I must stress that this viewpoint has its place in the life of the Church broadly considered, and is not necessarily excessively conservative. Indeed I must add that it plays not the least important of roles. However problems begin whenever what starts as a tendency, even a strongly felt one, becomes something exclusive. It then becomes captive to hidebound conservatism in all its forms. And this expresses itself in various ways.

Sometimes this is seen in a rooted attachment to traditional customs, loved for their own sake and not because they may help others. This often leads people to be blissfully unaware of the real problems which faith faces nowadays, Pitiless and unjust judgments are then passed, in the name of Christ, on those who are bringing the Gospel to bear on the issues affecting people who are trying to shape society. Their mistakes are loudly condemned and *in the world* is looked on as treachery and corruption.

Other people, milder in their approach, reach the position of looking on prayer as the only valid evangelical activity. Some charismatic groups run the risk of falling for this idea which, when it becomes exclusive, leads them to a sort of gnosticism. It represents an exaggerated view of *sedet ad dexteram Patris,* wherein the Spirit of the Lord exalted in glory is cut off from the Incarnation. The ways of salvation which such people adopt and try to promote are not bound up with great, liberating movements — movements leading people to greater dignity, truth and concord in mutual respect, or those which root out the spectre of injustice from the world. Rather are they produced in and for the community of the "initiated," where to bring a little piety and fervour to the world suffices. The life of faith becomes almost identical with piety and a pious life.

Now I want to be quite clear about this. There is nothing more normal than that a Christian should be tempermentally uneasy in an active life and feel called to a life of contemplation. If he or she refused this call, the Church would lose. When a community builds itself around a contemplative ideal, we should see in it a sign of the Spirit for which we should be grateful and to which we should give its due place. The Church, indeed, would not be what it is if there was no room for silence and long silences in its life, and we should pray that the wish for contemplation which is stirring in the churches will not die away. All this is a healthy sign but on one condition: the choice of such a life must be made with a feeling of sympathy, solidarity and fraternal prayer for those who are sweating blood as they work in the midst of the world, making all sorts of mistakes, but sticking at it for the sake of Christ. Failing this, one is no longer following the gospel but has slipped into gnosticism. To remain exclusively in the *not of the world* and confuse faith with pietism, to reduce the Christian mystery to *sedet ad dexteram Patris*, even in the name of an experience of the Spirit, is tantamount to condemning the faith to death.

The same must be said for the other kind of exclusive polarization — the abuse of *in the world.* Naturally an emphasis — even a strongly marked one — on deep involvement in working with modern society is not at all the same thing as the modernism and liberalism which the editors of some reviews have too quickly identified them with. But one is no longer following the Gospel when involvement amounts to complete assimilation without qualification, or when the Christian vocation is described only in terms of the action one is involved in (whether this be right-wing or left-wing), everything else in the faith being declared to be useless. This time what triumphs is *et incarnatus est.* There is no need for me to go back on this point which I have already dealt with at length. To reduce Christianity to involvement in efforts to help humanity take its destiny in hand, even in the name of the love of mankind and the service of history, is to smother the faith.

We must not conclude that living faith amounts to a happy mixture of incarnation and transcendence, action and piety. Just as there is no equilibrium, there is also no middle way, which indeed often equates with sheer mediocrity, nor is there any simple recipe. One must be *in the world* wherever God wills it and however deeply He wills it, whenever one's charism calls for it, and the circumstances demand it. But one must remain *before God* the while — a *before God* which is explicit and fills the heart.

We urgently need now to find out how to nourish this *before God*, and make it become part and parcel of our everyday existence. We are entering on a new stage of post-Council life, which will probably be dominated by a deepening of spiritual life. We must see that it will not constitute a retreat from what we have so courageously discovered with so much difficulty, but a real step forward. The charismatic renewal and the growing interest in prayer are important signs of a need which is being felt almost everywhere. But has the former always that grounding in faith which would allow us to look on it as a model? Has it not often become entangled in the mesh of a religiosity which is too fond of the marvellous to be at ease in the desert where faith inevitably leads a person, one day or another? As for the latter, has it yet found its authentic status?

# CHAPTER III

# Good News to the Poor

So that we might find our bearings as religious in the face of a world marked with suffering and evil and earnestly striving towards salvation, I described the truly evangelical tension between the notions of *in the world* and *not of the world*. This throws light on our mode of living and our involvement — however, we cannot leave the matter there if we want to live the faith with the theological realism which I have suggested, and without which we would no longer be true to the vocation of "following Christ." We must ask ourselves why it is that the covenant between God and the believer leads the latter to involve himself in situations where people are trying to change the world. There are still unanswered questions. Why, unlike most great religions, does Christianity send its "religious" into those parts of the world where the cry of misery is loudest? Why do the great renewal movements in the Church coincide with the rediscovery of the need to open one's eyes and heart once again to the suffering of the world? At a more profound level, why is it that while she proclaims her Lord to be a Lord of glory, the Church continues with such tenacity to venerate him on his Cross?

These are very important questions and, far from being abstract, can lead us to discover how *in the world* and *of the world* are linked together, and how, in the religious vocation, the gift of oneself to God is tied in with the giving of oneself to mankind. In a very down-to-earth way, this discovery brings us to the very heart of the drama of humanity.

## 1. God's Preference for the Poor

To all the questions I have asked there is only one answer, surprising and upsetting admittedly, but uncompromising, too. And all the more so in that it is closely linked to what the faith tells us of the very nature of God as revealed in Jesus Christ, for it describes God, not as the god of the deists, but first and foremost as gift and communion.

### IN HISTORY

The framework on which is built the adventure of God with his people, and which finds its high-point in the life of Jesus, and is continued in the history of the Church, is God's preference for the poor. This and this alone, it is becoming more and more important to add, allows the Church to become a powerful ferment in history, so much so that if the Church were to leave this aside, there would be nothing left but to declare officially that Christianity was dead.

### Messianism

There is an essential link between the undisputed fact that Christianity, like the Jewish faith from which it sprung, is a historical religion — that is to say, one which is based on a revelation perfected within a context of history that is intrinsically a part of universal history — and the fact that a believing people is a messianic people. In times like the present, when Christians are called on more and more to engage in discussions with Marxists of one kind or another, it is important to keep this in mind.

The faith, once it was revealed, burst upon the world as a mighty, hopeful force and wrote itself large among those movements which press history *forward* — towards a better future, towards a victory over whatever shadows the fate of mankind. Both Judaism and Christianity partake of the messianic spirit that is discernible throughout all human history, marshalling all the forces of life so that the hopes and dreams which lie buried in the human subconscious may triumph. For messianism is none other than the power which hope exerts, its hold on history and in history. This hope expresses itself in belief in a great awakening — in the coming of a time, ardently awaited and courageously prepared for, when the barriers against which we hurl ourselves will be swept away. Social and religious factors meet here, making each other fruitful. It is well known that this spirit of anticipation, of looking forward, is a principal element in the history both of groups and of individuals, above all when misfortune confronts them. It is this that keeps them from giving up the fight, with the bitter taste of defeat in their mouths. Judaism and Christianity have a common understanding of this.

A facile and romantic view of the Gospel law of love, coupled with an excessive valuing of generosity, too often makes people forget that Christianity is a faith that looks forward in hope, and that "love of one's neighbor" is sorely lacking if it is not associated in the closest way with "hope for mankind." Christianity lives and exerts all its power in the realization of this historical anticipation of better things, and in situations where messianic impulses have immemorially germinated. Christianity does not look on Christ only as the Savior of individuals individually; it is as *Gaudium et Spes* (No. 45) says: "the point at which the aims of history and of civilization converge." That *in the world* to which the *not of the world* engages itself is not something vague and indeterminate; it is marked by the longings and expectations, often violent, which have long troubled history.

Note that among the various titles given to the person of Jesus after the Resurrection, that of Messiah — Christ — became the most commonly used, and that His disciples

were named Christians because of this. The primitive
Church took up this title, which referred to the messianic expectations of a single community, but gave it an
interpretation which freed it from an exclusive link with
Israel and extended it to the whole of human history. Up to
that day when Christ "hands over the Kingdom to God the
Father" (I Cor 15:24), the Spirit of the Lord who is a
messianic Spirit, wills to be present in the longings of mankind, to make of their aspirations a fertile soil in which the
true hope which is the gift of Jesus Christ may germinate.
From its birth, and by its very nature, Christianity is messianic; hence inseparable from human hopes and expectations. And since these are at once spiritual and temporal,
individual and collective, historical and transcendent, it is
impossible to make a choice between a messianism which
looks only to eternal life and a messianism which is produc-
tive in history. There must be a symbiosis of the two.

Here we meet with that mysterious choice on God's part
—His preference for the poor, which is admittedly part and
parcel in a sense of messianism's very nature. For it is
obvious that the world of the poor, of second-class citizens,
of marginal and misunderstood people, is the culture-
medium out of which messianisms of the most varied sort
are produced, and that it so conditions those who dwell in it
that any inspiring ideal or heady scrap of rhetoric can
quickly set them ablaze. In our own time, the overturn in
China, the upsets in Latin America, and the rise of worker
movements, all bear witness to this. If it be true that the
progress of history is determined on the most obvious level
by rivalry among the powerful who are bent on domination,
it is also true that the realization of their plight by the mass
of the poor and oppressed encourages the projection of
utopian schemes for a better world and shocks people into
action on their behalf. Messiahs ordinarily gather the poor
around them. What else, for example, were the men and
women who followed Moses? It is in no way foreign to its
nature as a messianic people that the history of the people of
God at its origin, and again when it was reborn of the Spirit
at Pentecost, should be the history of a group of poor people

in whom faith in a Word had lighted a fire of hope and expectation.

What is the object of this hope? It tells us that a new state of things will come about, that a new era is in prospect. All humankind will be happy at last. There will be no more suffering. Justice will reign, peace will be established, and those whom chance or the malice of their fellow-creatures has reduced to misery will see the end of their troubles. So the prophets proclaimed, and at the end of the New Testament (in Chapter 21 of the Apocalypse) this promise of hope is repeated in the light of the mystery of Jesus. Every detail of it is repeated, and the context shows that Christian hope cannot be disjoined from the bitter experience of painful historical circumstances. "He will wipe away every tear from their eyes. Death will be no more. There will be no more mourning, nor outcries, nor suffering, for the world of the past has passed away. And He who sat upon the throne said: 'Behold, I make all things new.'" (Apoc 21: 4,5).

This is messianism in all its fullness. The God of Christians wills to uplift history and lead it towards a goal which He Himself has chosen for it. To this end, he makes use of a powerful force — the expectation of the poor. The promised newness of life is described in the words: liberation — justice — peace. We still await this new life, to be sure, and it is "transcendent" to our history — as we call it nowadays. Nevertheless, however transcendent it may be, it must be realized in our world — and not as some utopia of the future, but as something that has already taken place and is open to further development. As Jacques Maritain puts it in his *Christianisme et Democratie* (Paris, 1943, pages 50-51), "The good news which will open heaven and shows the way to eternal life requires also that the life of our earthly society be transformed to the very heart of its miseries and contradictions." And although the Kingdom of God is not of this earth: ". . . it must be prepared for, as best we can, amidst all the sorrows of earthly history."

It is the poor — in the widest sense of that term, not merely those in need of material things — whom this newness of life must benefit, first of all and immediately. The words of Matthew on the Last Judgment (Matt 25: 31-46), the letter of James (James 2: 1-13), and the summaries of the Acts of the Apostles bear witness to this.

## Why does God Prefer the Poor?

But why does God prefer the poor? It cannot be because this is the nature of messianism, that would be to beg the question. Neither can it be explained by a romantic fancy of the goodness of the poor, as if these were better than other people and necessarily nearer God. It is obvious that there are bad poor people just as there are good rich people and a dispassionate examination will discover amongst the poor the same mixture of moral grandeur and misery which is the common lot of mankind. Why then does God prefer the poor? Simply because God is God. The ideal of the kings of Israel has a bearing here. As the foremost duty of the king was to see that justice was done to all his subjects, and since, in the normal course of events, the powerful continually exploited the weak, the king had to defend the weak and see that they were given their due rights. As he is a just king, God must prefer the poor, and be on their side. He owes this to himself, to his divine justice, and to his greatness as God — "to the honour of His Kingdom." In this way will history be set right.

Biblical messianism takes its origins here. It springs from the mysterious conjunction between God and the dreams, utopias and aspirations which are born of poverty. God is on the side of the poor simply because he is God. He does not love the poor "the way English old ladies love lost cats", as Bernardos says in *Journal d'un curé de campagne*. He loves them with the love of a God who is just. And Luke says just this when, in his version of the Beatitudes, he describes Jesus proclaiming "blessed" not the "poor in spirit" but simply the poor — those who have to deal with material or psychological misery and want, those who are suffering, those who feel the acid burning of despair, those who may be well-off but are tortured by unbearable distress.

They are "blessed" not because they are virtuous, and still

less because they are suffering, but quite simply because God is for them.

And this is why, in the biblical recommendation to hope, the Messiah addresses Himself first of all to the poor. His recognition of them will be a sign that the Kingdom of God is at hand. This is just what Jesus did: "Go back and tell John what you have seen and heard; the blind see again, the lame walk, lepers are cleansed, and the deaf hear, the dead are raised to life, the Good News is proclaimed to the poor" (Luke 7:22 and cp. Matt 11:4-5). It is easier now to understand the little phrase in the Acts of the Apostles which describes the state of the primitive community, acting under the Spirit of Christ: "None of their members was ever in want" (Acts 4:34). Since the dawn of the Kingdom is already bright, and what was longed for has been found, there must be no more poverty. God's plan for history and the aspirations of the poor draw together at this point.

## ORIGIN AND FORM OF THE APOSTOLIC RELIGIOUS VOCATION

Let us pause here and recall our reflections on the *in the world* quality of a living faith as part of the vocation of following Christ. It is no chance happening that the apostolic religious life, throughout its history, has made care for the poor a constituent element. The "world" in which religious propose to follow Christ is not a static, abstract notion but the very concrete world wherein history is lived out under God. In it, religious constitute what may be called "God's party." Now for those of the Christian faith, to consider the relationship of God with the world is to think, first of all, of God's relationship with the poor — that word to be taken in its widest sense, and not limited to any special kind of poverty or to any particular social class. Furthermore, to think of the poor in terms of God's relationship to them must be to think of God's relationship to *all* who seek salvation or strive for a better time to come — not just those who organize to achieve such ends and are able to do so. If there are political implications in the Gospel's message of hope — and this can in no way be overlooked or dismissed —it is also true that the Gospel goes much further than mere politics, and that politics is not its first consideration. "Everything has a political angle," so the slogan goes — but to this the faithful Christian replies, "Politics is not the whole of mankind's being."It is a means or tool to be employed in the working-out of the historical plan for the human family. Biblical messianism goes beyond political messianisms, be they of the left-wing variety or the right. The *in the world* in which religious become involved is the world in which poor people toil and hope. And the intimations of the Kingdom which religious effect in it are those acts which give reality to God's preference for the poor. No hard-and-fast distinctions can be made between good and bad poor people, for this would be to regard some of them as dead-weight, fit only to be rejected in anger or disgust. This would be quite contrary to God's attitude. He supports the weak, whom the powerful despise.

It is all the more important to stress all this at a time when a number of Western societies are beginning to question the primacy of politics and political action. While admitting the essential and unique role of politics in the development of society, people are becoming keenly aware of the dangers in centralized, bureaucratic power and fearful of what future perils may lurk in the over-politicization of our world. Social life has a necessary political dimension, but this must be seen clearly as a part of something greater than itself. The true and proper aims of society cannot be crudely identified with political maneuverings. Politics must be subordinated to a wider vision of the social vocation of mankind.

## THE INCARNATION: GOD MADE POOR

God's preference for the poor goes beyond His willing to open up for them the ways of justice. Its nature is fully revealed in the mystery of Jesus. And here we are at the very heart of the Gospel.

He whom the Resurrection was to reveal as the Messiah —the Christ — who came to fulfill all human expectations, is the Son of God, exalted at the right hand of the Father. He is this, however, because He made the human condition of poverty His own and lived it right up to the final, anguished humiliation of the Cross. The Incarnation is the mystery of God Himself in the mystery of one poor man.

We must firmly reject the superficial, although still common opinion which holds that Jesus' poverty was a deliberate ascetic exercise. How many misleading interpretations have been given to the verse: "The Son of Man has nowhere to lay His head!" Jesus was not poor because He was born of poor parents, or because He chose to live a life of austerity. We know nothing of the circumstances of His family, and He does not appear to have led as austere a life as John the Baptist. Nor was His relationship with the poor simply a matter of His championing their cause and performing works of mercy and kindness for them as witness to His Gospel. His link with all poor persons is infinitely more profound.

Jesus is God *made* poor, because on His Cross (and culminating in the Resurrection, which set the seal on His belonging to the mystery of God), He made the condition of mankind in its most tragic aspects His own. Consider the anguished cry in the Garden of Olives — the appeal to the Father from the cross — the death between two thieves on the hill of shame at the city gate! This was the real death of a defenseless man; the real breaking of a man at the brink of despair; the real crucifixion of a man rejected. This was the very fulfillment of the Beatitudes as they were understood by St. Luke. The poor are not only the privileged people of the new era, but the event which brought this into being came from one of themselves. The goal of messianic hopes, towards which faith leads the desire of the poor for liberation and their cries for help, is the work of a "poor man" like themselves but a "poor man" who in the very depths of his being is God himself. God's choice of the poor is so complete and absolute that he does not limit himself to being God-for-the-poor or even God-with-the-poor, but in Jesus God-was-made-poor. It is here alone that the Incarnation reveals its true meaning and its deep-seated roots in the reality of human history. The ultimate victory of the poor is that they bring history to its fulfillment. Even the rich will owe their happiness in the Kingdom to a "poor man," a "rejected man" called Jesus. And the great stream of tradition has understood the cross in just this way; for going beyond the literal meaning of Luke's words, it has rightly extended Jesus' words: "Happy are the poor; they have given the Messiah to the world, the Savior to those who were waiting, the goal to those who were living in hope." But all this *on account of* God, because his mysterious choice fell on them.

Here we seem to be at the very heart of the Gospel, face to face with a fathomless mystery but one secretly linked, for all that, with the drama of human history. For justice, as God sees it, goes far beyond our human notions and approaches what John calls *agape*. The poor do not come into their own just for themselves; since the magnanimous and unimaginable action by which God, through Jesus, becomes one with them and associates them with his Kingdom, opens to all the human family a way to reach the hoped-for goal. We begin to see that our following Christ *in the world* —and, as I have pointed out, *in the world* as marked with the hopes and desires of the poor—cannot but be deeply affected by what I have just been talking about.

We must not beat around the bush but boldly affirm that in the present situation, our religious congregations will never know renewal unless they share God's preference for the poor. And every word of this counts, as we can easily see, for it is not just *for the poor* but also *God's preference*. It is not just short-term generosity looking for quick results, but an attitude that affects the history of mankind. This is the point where *in the world* and *not of the world* as they affect our vocation and involvement, meet together, as do the relevance and the *before God* of our faith. The meeting point is the poor.

## "FOLLOWING CHRIST"

All this sheds light on the basic meaning of the vocation of "following Christ." The mystery of Jesus is woven together with the mystery of the poor. But since the purpose of the Incarnation is essentially messianic, Jesus' link with the poor and the weak is not simply aimed at changing their situation, rather it is a fundamental sharing in that situation, a sharing in which the apparently futile happening of the Cross is the high-point and the most perfect sign. In Jesus' choice of the poor and the weak, which is also the incarnation of God's choice, there is, then, a gratuitous dimension, contemplative rather than active in the sense that contemplation implies being caught up in a mystery and converted by it, heart and soul. The Cross is a sharing in human distress. Concentrating too closely on the problem of the expiatory values of the Passion, Western theology (both Catholic and Reformed) sees it all in terms of efficaciousness and redemption whose effects must be measured. It leaves aside, sometimes almost completely, the notion of "God's compassion" for human poverty, which after all is the first element of the Cross. John's first letter says, in a stunningly simple sentence: "This has taught us love — that he gave up his life for us" (1 John 11:16 and cp. 4:10). The gift of life is more important than anything else! Salvation has come about when the seed of *agape* — the love of God himself — was sown in the soil of human misery. Otherwise it would only be generosity — divine alms-giving. If it is true to say that the Incarnation is aimed at Redemption, one must hasten to add that there is no salvation apart from the Incarnation.

The "following of Christ," according to which a man or woman makes a radical decision to come to grips with the call of the Gospel, is profoundly affected by the place held by communion with the poor and the weak in the mystery of Jesus. The great pillars of religious life, which for centuries have been called the three vows, find their meaning here and here alone. Their purpose is to lead people to share in this poverty. As against a theological tendency, which is not well founded in tradition, and which (in a rather esthetic way) centers everything on chastity, or — as is glibly said "celibacy for the sake of the Kingdom," the classical three vows should be seen as a progress towards poverty. The poverty of self-assertion and the search for personal power (the vow of obedience); the poverty of ownership of goods (the vow of poverty; the poverty of the flesh (the vow of chastity) — these vows of religion are not straightaway aimed at a moral goal, nor can they be understood as a desire to be generous which becomes heroic if need be. Rather are they to effect the actualization of poverty which forms the first stage of Jesus' sharing in God's preference for the poor. It is in this way that they have the theological value without which they would no longer be evangelical.

## Unity of Vows and Apostolic Action

It is precisely here that the unity between religious vows and apostolic action is seen, for it is clear that for a religious, as for Jesus, sharing in God's choice calls for action, for specific involvement in liberation movements or in efforts to bring about more justice. I have insisted that no limit can be put to the extent and seriousness of this involvement. However, we must be honest and clear-headed about this. Usually, Christians find themselves taking part in already existing movements, though these movements may be the surfacing of Gospel springs which have run underground for centuries. The involvement of the Church in the search for social justice is an obvious example. The emancipation of various social groups, among whom religious were exercising their apostolate, can be seen to be perfectly in harmony with the Gospel even though it did not necessarily owe its origin to it.

If one is to be truly evangelical, solidarity with the poor in one's life-style is of prime importance — a spiritual communion with the Beatitude of the poor, whose great witness is Francis of Assisi. For who would deny that Francis, as Charles de Foucauld more recently, has helped to free the poor? I would go as far as to say that he implanted in our Western world a sense of unease which has produced more results than all the "exterior works of charity" carried out just to help others. As M. D. Chenu says:

"If Francis of Assisi caused such a shock to Christendom that it changed its structures, this was not primarily because he attacked the vice of selfish hoarding of riches, but because, breaking though the barriers and privileges of the feudal system, he cleared a way for the elementary law of fraternity.... By its simple purity, Franciscan fraternity gives spiritual meaning and evangelical values to that human emancipation whose immediate causes were industrial expansion and better circulation of capital. (*Paradoxe de la pauvreté evangelique et construction du monde.*)

We should reflect deeply on this point in these days when the numerous calls on our time, the hurly-burly of activities, the surfeit of mass media, are in danger of making us forget, or even think little of, the evangelical values of being one with Christ, the Servant, in God's preference for the poor and simple. Our religious profession accomplished this in us before we became involved *in the world*. Apostolic religious life finds its foundation in this, and also the source of its renewal.

It is for this reason too that contemplatives and hermits have a part to play in the apostolate. Even if they do not join in mass movements that shake up the social scene, or become involved in the active apostolate, they can (insofar as they try collectively and individually to remain faithful to their call to be detached) be witnesses to the mysterious choice of God *made* poor. In this way they "actualize" the fundamental mystic dimension of the involvement of God, and of the Church, *in the world*. Think again of Francis, of a really poor and simple Poor Clare convent in a town. They bear witness, of course, to *not of the world* — but *not of the world* as part of the Incarnation of the Father's Son *in* His weakness. All religious life, however apostolic it is, must be signed with this mystic dimension if it is to be an authentic "following of Christ."

Understood in this way, the religious profession also throws a searching light on apostolic action. There is nothing worse than generosity for muddled reasons, nothing more dangerous than uncritical acceptance of worldly points of view. But Francis' evangelical poverty, and — wherever it is rightly lived — the fidelity of religious to their profession, are powerful inducements to clear thinking for those who generously want to become involved in the great movements which are changing our society. What is the ideal for which we are aiming? In our Western world there is a way of looking at progress, propagated by the mass media and preached by false prophets, which corresponds in fact to a step towards destruction and the enslavement of mankind. One type of alienation is to be exchanged for another. And where indeed can that true freedom be found, without which one loses one's dignity and slumps into an empty gratification which slowly eats one away? The Gospel can have no truck with any ideal of social life centered almost exclusively on material objects and which all shades of political opinion play up to. Of itself, then, apostolic generosity is not enough to enable one to live evangelically the *in the world* quality of the religious vocation. A sort of apostolic vigilance is also needed to see that in the flurry of political and trade union business, the spirit of riches does not get the better of the spirit of poverty. By setting the seal of the Gospel on one's flesh, one's self-assertion, and one's desire to possess, the vows of religion are a realistic principle of judgment, immanent in generosity and guiding it by a sort of instinct.

## To Be Christlike

Such is the "Following of Christ," if we look at it, not as a moral code but as a striving to be Christlike. Religious of all kinds, by their very existence, from their way of living their profession of poverty-chastity-obedience on to their involvement in the lot of mankind, are partakers of the mystery of God's choice of the poor, which is the basis of the mission of Jesus and the Church. Living and acting are in continual osmosis here. Especially today the *in the world* to which the Spirit leads them is the *in the world* of the poor and the simple — in which biblical hope took seed and germinated, and in which the Christ of God took flesh. If they want to remain faithful to their calling they too must take flesh *in the world* of the poor. That is where they belong.

Need I repeat that by poor I do not mean simply those who have nothing? Poverty has a much wider meaning than that. The disproportion in life-styles of different social classes has produced "relative poverty," the poverty of those who do not lack the necessities of life but cannot be content, and feel deprived of their rights when they realize that the fruit of their hard work goes to others. The Gospel can certainly conduce to sound judgment in this regard, for this new kind of poverty is little different from that of the simple and weak, incapable of achieving their rights unaided, and whom the Bible calls the poor. This is where religious find their role. As I have remarked more than once, it is not simply a question of serving the poor, working for them, striving might and main for the victory of fundamental human rights, or taking part in development programs. One must have, deep-down, something of the attitude of Francis of Assisi: the desire to let poverty wash off on oneself, not to be afraid to become poor oneself. This is where we will find the Gospel.

## CHRISTIANITY AND FORMS OF MARXISM

What we have been considering here should help us to face up to the problem of Marxism. There is no escaping the fact that the "Grand Inquisitor" for Western Christianity is no longer atheism but the Marxist ideology. In the years to come, if they are truly committed to the cause of the poor, religious will be drawn into a confrontation of their faith with one or another brand of Marxism — and this, both as individuals and as communities. A prospect full of difficulties! For Marxism is messianic, and Berdiaeff is correct in asserting (with a number of qualifications) that it belongs basically to the Christian era of history and carries an eschatological element which is rooted in Revelation. Marxism has hidden affinities with Christianity, and that is why a Christian who is more than marginally acquainted with his own faith finds that he cannot reply to the several forms of Marxism with a simple "yes" or "no." He wavers between "yes...but" and "no...but." He is also quite aware that the Marxist engagement on behalf of the exploited is — to every honest believer — "a testimony to a duty unfulfilled, and to a task that Christianity left unrealized." The Christian conscience cannot simply ignore Marxism or push it aside. Rather, Christianity must question it — and be questioned by it. The astonishing flowering of the apostolate which, especially since World War II, has led the Church to reassume its responsibility to work for the removal of injustice would not have come about as it has but for the stimulus of Marxism. On the other hand, Marxism seems to Christians to be a fragment of the Gospel from which essential parts are lacking, which makes it at the same time in tune and out of tune with the Christian faith. When confronted by Marxism, a Christian experiences an odd mixture of understanding and unease — the unease coming mainly from the Marxist refusal to allow any place for God. And is it not the specific task of religious to bear witness to God in the Church and *in the world*? Not to the God of the deists, but to the God who in Jesus Christ has revealed His visage precisely by His choosing the poor — and, indeed, in that very choice itself?

## 2. *The Hope of the Poor, the Source of Salvation*

> Desire by definition is selfish and tends toward possession. The other is considered only in relation to myself, to the pleasure he/she can bring me if I am concupiscent, or simply in relation to the services he/she can do for me. Hope, on the other hand, is unselfish. To hope, as I have written in my *Homo Viator*, is always to hope for us. (Gabriel Marcel, *Présence et Immortalité*, Paris, 1968, p. 248).

The above lines by Marcel lead us to a more profound and even more disturbing signification of God's preference for the poor which, as we have seen, is the origin and determining factor of the religious call to "follow Christ." God's taking part in the hopes of the poor, as realized on the Cross of Christ, is the source of the salvation not only of the poor but of all people. His choice of the poor is His choice also of charity for the rich. Even though their sinfulness is sometimes denounced in the strongest of terms, they are not excluded from the redemption and consigned to damnation. However (and herein is the paradox of the Gospel), in the Kingdom of God the situation is reversed; the rich are debtors to those whose masters they were in the world. They are called, in Christ, to share in a salvation given to the world by the poor. The word "rich", I hasten to say, must be taken in the broad sense. Just as poor people are not simply those who have no material possessions, so also the rich are not just those who are well provided with the world's goods. Their state of mind exists even among those who are most in want, and "the wretched fellow who is sleeping off a drunk beside a stream is dreaming, perhaps, the same dreams as Caesar asleep beneath his bed-curtains of imperial purple." (George Bernanos, *Journal d'un curé de campagne*)

## MESSIANIC RECONCILIATION

In the plan of salvation, the poor become lords of the rich and mighty because of Jesus, the Poor Man, made Lord by His cross. This is not vengeance but reconciliation. The Gospel sees no opposition between the victory of the poor and the law of reconciliation, one implying the other; but the reconciliation must not be thought of as something purely in the moral order. Such a perspective misrepresents the mystery of the cross. It is not a question of generosity but of *agape*. From the time of the crucifixion, there has existed an objective forgiveness that precedes and qualifies every subjective forgiveness — a pardon given by an action which every other action must take as its model. This is the great pardon of the Poor Man who opens His Kingdom to those who, sometimes without being able to do otherwise, and often not understanding the implications of what they do (being blinded by the society in which they live), do their best to keep Him poor and make little of Him. The messianic reconciliation — longed-for throughout the Bible — centers upon the fact that in Jesus it is the poor who will save the rich, the despised and oppressed who will make the Kingdom come.

However, since the Resurrection the Kingdom has *already* begun to come into the world, any efforts to throw off the yoke of injustice — even struggles to change conditions which hold people down and are managed by the powerful — are already a gift of salvation for the rich to the degree that their consciences are awakened, and that they are led to behave with respect for their own humanity. By liberating themselves, the poor open the way to salvation to the rich as well; by compelling the rich to recognize their dignity as human beings, they bring about a renewal in the rich of a sense of that same dignity in themselves. The famous text of Matthew 25 on the eschatological judgment can be understood in this sense; although it does not correspond literally, neither does such a reading pervert the text. In taking a proper attitude towards the poor, every human being *already* meets with the Son of Man and His pardon.

This eschatological pardon — this reconciliation of the Day of the Son of Man — which brings out powerfully and in its true dimension the objective pardon and reconciliation of the cross, has a practical application in the evangelical command to love and respect one's enemy. Here again is a case where we must not trifle with the Gospel's message or try to argue our way around it. The evangelical impact of the Sermon on the Mount is clearly observed in this command, with its *not of the world* quality so strongly in contrast with worldly wisdom. However, it is here that — *in the world* —the Gospel introduces a value proper to itself. Reconciliation is the reality (already granted objectively in Jesus Christ) which through all its history the Christian community, living *in the world* as it does, has been charged to effect and preach. It is true that this is no easy task, and that in certain circumstances it can be more an ardent commitment carried on in suffering than a success even in prospect. Yet Christians must always aim at it. This does not mean, of course, that the poor must meanwhile bear the brunt, or that one should settle for lame compromises in practical situations. The requirement of reconciliation does not do away with the requirement of justice. *In the world* and *not of the world* meet at the coming-together of these two requirements, as at a crossroads; neither is to be neglected, as the Gospel makes clear.

Religious who are deeply involved in efforts to change society will find this a major responsibility. I do not think it an exaggeration to say that for many of them who have made common cause with a social group, a type of labor, or in general with the working class, this is probably the most demanding but also the most specifically Christian aspect of their commitment. The *before God* quality of profession proves itself in this desire for reconciliation, detracting in no way from the gift of oneself in the cause of justice, leading to no disloyalty to the group among whom one finds oneself, but preventing one from seeing in another group, another class, and above all in another person, an object of hatred or contempt. It is here, perhaps, that the openness to universal brotherhood which is supposed to follow from the vow of chastity may make its presence felt. Even if it be hard for either side in a controversy to make any outward gesture of appeasement because it would appear a kind of treachery, even if an antagonism is so strong that it would appear hypocritical to offer a hand in friendship, a religious cannot accept the simple view that the opponent is nothing but a liar, or the pitiful victim of a false ideology, or an exploiter, or a rabid anarchist. I hasten to add that this holds good for both sides, for the left as well as the right — and indeed within the Church also. The splintering of the Christian community, resulting from pressure by groups on left or right and the confusion over pluralism and division, is so much at odds with the Gospel that the Church is slowly losing credibility, and the faith that she preaches its relevance. Enthusiasm for the temporal struggle, solidarity with fellow workers whoever they may be, cannot, according to the spirit of the Gospel, be allowed to take precedence over communion with believers.

This attitude of reconciliation must also be displayed outside the Christian community, in society at large. Can any religious be said to follow Christ in all sincerity, so long as he or she stifles the impulse to strive towards any true reconciliation in which the demands of justice are met, and the wish to lead towards it those people with whom they are involved? It may well be that the bad example of the power struggles going on all around us has left us open to a temptation to Manicheism, which inclines us to see in our opponents — whatever they may do — the very incarnation of evil. Conditions of injustice arise more often from social structures than from those people who, for various reasons, support those structures. Nonetheless, we continue to look on this one or that one among our opponents as a man or woman who is suspect.

## THE CHURCH AND THE RICH

More than ever nowadays, congregations and communities have a duty also to look after the rich, and indeed many of their members are engaged in an apostolate to them. For it would be quite wrong and contrary to the Gospel to equate preference for the poor with rejection of the rich who are to be left to their fate. Our general chapters will soon have to face up to the fact that the faith is waning in a number of influential quarters. If it is true that some social groups back away from the renewal of the Church and are much more inclined to a nostalgia for the past, is the fault to be laid only at their doors? Have we ourselves not failed to bring them to a proper understanding of God's preference for the poor? Is not the evangelisation of the rich part of the reconciliation offered to all by the cross? Even if an immense amount of patience and tact is needed — as is also the case in much of the world of the poor — we cannot accept that the efforts of the Church to foster love of the poor should produce such bitter fruit as the loss of precisely those people whom the Gospel says the poor will save.

An important obligation faces us here. The Church must try to convert the rich to the mystery of God, as revealed in the Scriptures. If by disputing the present-day social system the poor lead the rich to examine their consciences, it is up to believers to see that the results of this examination will lead them to the Gospel. The sign that our society is a perverted one is not, in fact, that thousands of people are demanding more justice and uniting to struggle for their rights, but rather the fact that the rich have become proud —that is to say, "people who have power over others, who manipulate them, despise them, and make decisions for them." And this remains true even when the rich were poor themselves only yesterday. Although the truly great man is the poor man who fights to remove from the earth that injustice which warps the mind even of the rich who rob them of honor, it is also true that our society is built on the greatness of the rich. Still and all, Dominic was nobler than his neighbour the rich Cistercian abbot, and the misery of poor countries is nobler than the tragic riches of our sur- feited societies. As Francois Perroux well says, the spirit of the Beatitudes "dishonours money." The Spirit of "follow- ing Christ" urges us neither to run away from the rich nor to capitulate to them and accept their views, but rather to work hard to convert them to the evangelical mystery of the poor. This goes much deeper than a call for social justice and for respect for the rights of everyone to the fruits of his labor. It includes also an evangelical recognition of the roles played by the poor in the salvation of the world. In light of this, the kiss given to the leper is not an act of virtue or courage but of truth. And it is to this truth that, as religious, we have to lead all people, the rich included. The necessary involvement to work for justice is the *in the world* quality of this truth; the kiss for the leper is its *not of the world* quality. Then, and then only can we judge ourselves faithful to the call to witness to the Gospel *in the world.*

## SPIRITUAL POVERTY

Whether they throw themselves heart-and-soul into working for the poor or courageously attempt to teach the rich the place of the poor in God's plan, it is obvious that religious must act as poor-people-according-to-Christ. For the "following of Christ," which is their precise form of life, implies that they share His outlook, Who, being poor, saved all mankind.

This means that their poverty in which, as I have said, the triple consecration — obedience-poverty-chastity — finds its unity is not simply poverty in the social sense, but is profoundly affected by its dependence on Jesus Christ. The nakedness of the cross shows the unbreakable link between human poverty and the gratuitousness of God's grace. It also shows that the person who is poor in Christ does not put his hope in human strength, however well adapted this is to solve the problems which haunt our society. The messianism of the cross is a messianism of grace. In his version of the Beatitudes — which is different from Luke's — Matthew calls this poverty "poverty of spirit," "poverty of the heart." For our hope must be fixed on God, and not on the powers of this world. The exegetes point out that throughout the Passion story the Gospels underline this attitude of Jesus regarding the authorities who will decide his fate. In the Old Testament, the poor of Yahweh — the *anawim* whose faith is handed on to us by the prophets and the psalms — also opted for faithfulness to the promise of the living God and refused to put their trust in the power who at that time controlled the world.

Spiritual poverty, then, has a role to play in the development of history. By means of spiritual poverty, in the midst of conflicts which shape the course of history and often result simply in swapping one kind of domination for another, the people of God refuse to tie human hope to the powers of this world, be they political or spiritual. The people of God refuse to allow the powers of this world to control people's consciences as if their ideologies infallibly shaped the course of history and represented the only valid explanation of mankind. For through faith, the people know that even if they include elements necessary for "happiness," and even if their political plans are useful for the progress of humanity, whenever the plans of the powerful become absolute and domineering, they trample on and thwart the hopes of mankind.

The ideal the Gospel sets before us is not just that of a person who is happy, but rather that of a person who is blessed, and this changes completely one's attitude to the forces imminent in history.

> "We do not want to curtail people's comfort but rather to open up the city to the presence of God and to the miracle of His Incarnation, whose purpose is not to make men "happy" but "blessed," matured by the sun of the Beatitudes even though they are persecuted and martyred ... Everything is subordinated to the Kingdom and not just to the natural development of the earth, or even to the peaceful unrolling of history, but to their transfiguration into the "new earth" there is to be no avoiding responsibilities or taking refuge in the next life, but a change in aim: the changing of the values of the second last chapter of history into those of the last and final one." (P. Evdokimov, *L'amour fou de Dieu*, p. 141)

The search for justice, liberation and progress does not automatically lead to that goal towards which Christian hope says mankind is tending. For this goal is not to be won through social struggle or economic and political development. It is achieved only through the evangelical *metanoia* which, though it may involve these struggles and developments, is never limited to them.

All this gives rise to tension. Though a Christian realizes that people must work for justice and fraternity in this world, and that everyone must do his or her level best to bring about the petition of the Our Father: "Thy will be done on earth as it is in heaven," a person cannot accept the possibility of an earthly paradise to be accomplished in this life. In other words, faith teaches him that people do not go from happiness to Beatitude and that the latter (understood in the Christian sense) is not the result of the former (in the

ordinary sense of the word). So, in the light of the Beatitudes, a person feels one must criticize any effort, however
admirable, to attain earthly happiness, whenever this is
understood in an absolute sense, which would rule out its
relationship with Beatitude. This is especially relevant when
we consider the temptation which weighs down our society:

> This is the temptation of ample possessions and the joy
> of being alive, the temptation of someone who has con-
> trol of his life, his property, his destiny, and who owes
> nothing to anybody except himself, his own strength and
> the power of his arm. Or perhaps he depends on those
> false gods, easily managed and complacent, who at the
> price of a few sacrifices and observances, guarantee life,
> security, health and the possession of the earth. To the
> person who is affected by it, this will not appear to be a
> temptation at all: for him it is reality, life, matter-of-fact
> and actual. And he would laugh at the notion of tempta-
> tion." (O. du Roy, *Moines d'aujourd'hui*, p. 250)

This also demands the existence of an authentic spiritual
freedom.

## SPIRITUAL FREEDOM

Here again, the link between "following Christ" and the
way in which the vows make the religious face up to the
problems of possession and of power is high-lighted. What
is true for all Christians is true — in a special way — for
those who make profession of "following Christ." Where
they are most involved in trying to improve the lot of
mankind, they must introduce a note of anxiety. We may
even say —though it is an unhappy phrase and sounds bad,
especially today — they are never unconditional allies.
Their involvement with a group cannot mean a complete
acceptance of what the group accepts as its aims and hopes.
They will work honestly; they will strive for the cause; but
they reserve the right to say "no". The faith understands this
"no" as the safeguard of human hope. And far from being a

refusal to serve, it represents the "no" of poverty which guarantees salvation. It takes its origin in the "no" Jesus said to the powers of this world and also of his own people. So it can lead to the cross, and in our days baptized people of all denominations, and religious, too, are experiencing this in dictatorships of the right and the left, in regimes which use the forms of Christianity to keep the *status quo*, and also in regimes which employ Marxist ideology to stamp out freedom. These martyrs — who are linked with Christ the Suffering Servant — have a prophetic value, not only for the Church but also for the world. Martyrdom cuts across the everyday world and proclaims a new beginning. And why? Simply because it is the supreme example of poverty, and because on account of God's choice it is the poor who guarantee the salvation of the world.

I used the present tense: "they are never unconditionally allies," "they reserve the right to say "no." It would perhaps have been more correct to have used the imperative. However this would have smacked of power rather than poverty, and we must preach by example! During the coming years, I think that we religious will have to train ourselves in this way, to liberty. We have succeeded very well in doing this in other fields, since we started on our renewal chapters, and why should we not do the same here? We will have to learn at times how to say "no," and this, as a result of our faith, not out of fear. And we will have every right to say this "no" on account of our active and honest involvement, and because it is not meant as a kind of excommunication. It will be a "no" pronounced *in the world* by a faith, living and relevant on account of being *not of the world*. This is a serious problem with many implications. Are we going to submit to the powerful — who are not necessarily the wealthy but often those who are rich in the power of persuasion — and give up preaching messianic hope? If so, we have nothing to say to the world. Because we lack the spiritual poverty which refuses to be browbeaten by what is fashionable, we will have destroyed true hope. And we will have made ourselves redundant, not on account of poverty, but by cowardice.

# Conclusion

I must now try to draw some conclusions. At the beginning I asked a question. How can religious, who tend more and more to be involved in working in the world, find the bearings of their faith in the society which is ours? Are there not many ideologies at work in this society, which often produce more interesting results than does Christian teaching, as it is lived and sometimes defended in fear and dread of the world? I asked an even more serious question, which troubles many people even though they are afraid to express it out loud: have we any place in a world where everything revolves around socio-economic problems, and where the struggle for power has become the major factor for so many people who are working for the good of society? Is the apostolic type of religious life going to become a thing of the past and be replaced by secular institutes (more in keeping with *in the world*) and contemplative orders (more in keeping with *not of the world*)?

## TO FALL IN LINE WITH GOD'S PREFERENCE FOR THE POOR

The answer I have suggested is only a pointer, and will not allay every worry. It is not an easy one to accept, but it does throw a certain light and may help us take a quiet look at the situation in which we find ourselves. I think we can say that we have discovered a foundation for our evangelical vocation to "follow Christ" which will put it in line with the movements stirring our Western societies, and enable us to take a fresh look at it, without betraying either the Gospel or our own age.

In its fundamental notion and structures — especially the three main roots which are obedience, poverty and chastity — "following Christ" implies a sharing in God's preference for the poor, i.e., those to whom justice must be done and those who have to deal with one or another kind of misfortune. But are not the search for justice and the struggles for freedom from all that oppresses people the very things for which generous people are striving today? "Following Christ" and sharing his preference for the poor, therefore, make us share straight away in the great movements of our time. The *in the world* quality of the faith, the place where it becomes relevant and can thus challenge our contemporaries, is *in the world* which is torn by suffering, and tragedies, tears but also is stirring with the hopes of the little, the weak and the oppressed. The striving towards more justice and a greater development of the potentialities of our society, can serve very well, then, as the place where our faith can become actual and real. And we must be brave about this, remembering that faith is always influenced by the times in which we live. Otherwise it would be neither living nor capable of spreading.

## THE MYSTICAL DIMENSION

In God's preference for the poor, as accomplished in Jesus, there is also a mystical dimension, a *not of the world* quality which is just as important as the other. Jesus is not only the person who serves the poor and shows them the infinite mercy of the Father towards them, making them see that He is on their side. He is also the person who, on His cross, assumes the human condition in all its tragedy, and from His sharing in poverty sets the course of the salvation of mankind. On account of this, the faithfulness of a religious to his profession, urging him to live as Christ lived, is of capital importance. Something of the life of Francis of Assisi or of Charles de Foucauld, with its prophetic value, is present in every religious life.

In this way the courageous efforts of religious working *in the world*, with their inevitable social and political dimensions, take on something of Christ's acceptance of poverty. On the one hand they will not confuse working for the poor with rejecting the rich; rather, they will try to open for the rich the way to salvation given by the poor. On the other hand, they are able to say "no" to whatever would limit human hope to goals which are not compatible with the vocation of a person as the faith understands it. And by trying to live this evangelical call *before God*, the religious realizes that he or she is serving God himself or herself by following Jesus, the Servant of the Father.

Can we not in this way achieve unity in our life?

Can we not in this way achieve unity in our presence in the world as well as in our belonging to the God of Jesus Christ?

It is for us to seize the opportunity.

# DATE DUE

|  |  |  |  |
|--|--|--|--|
|  |  |  |  |
|  |  |  |  |
|  |  |  |  |
|  |  |  |  |
|  |  |  |  |
|  |  |  |  |
|  |  |  |  |
|  |  |  |  |
|  |  |  |  |
|  |  |  |  |
|  |  |  |  |
|  |  |  |  |
|  |  |  |  |
|  |  |  |  |
|  |  |  |  |
|  |  |  |  |
|  |  |  |  |
|  |  |  |  |